LIVES OF GREAT RELIGIOUS BOOKS

The Book of *Revelation*

LIVES OF GREAT RELIGIOUS BOOKS

The Book of *Revelation*, Timothy Beal
The *Dead Sea Scrolls*, John J. Collins
The *Bhagavad Gita*, Richard H. Davis
John Calvin's *Institutes of the Christian Religion*, Bruce Gordon
The *Book of Mormon*, Paul C. Gutjahr
The Book of *Genesis*, Ronald Hendel
The *Book of Common Prayer*, Alan Jacobs
The Book of *Job*, Mark Larrimore
The *Koran* in English, Bruce B. Lawrence
The *Lotus Sūtra*, Donald S. Lopez Jr.
The Tibetan Book of the Dead, Donald S. Lopez Jr.
C. S. Lewis's *Mere Christianity*, George M. Marsden
Dietrich Bonhoeffer's *Letters and Papers from Prison*, Martin E. Marty
Thomas Aquinas's *Summa theologiae*, Bernard McGinn
The *I Ching*, Richard J. Smith
The *Yoga Sutras of Patanjali*, David Gordon White
Augustine's *Confessions*, Garry Wills
The *Talmud*, Barry Wimpfheimer

FORTHCOMING

The Book of *Exodus*, Joel Baden
Confucius's *Analects*, Annping Chin and Jonathan D. Spence
The *Autobiography* of Saint Teresa of Avila, Carlos Eire
Josephus's *The Jewish War*, Martin Goodman
Dante's *Divine Comedy*, Joseph Luzzi
The Greatest Translations of All Time: The *Septuagint* and the *Vulgate*,
    Jack Miles
The Passover *Haggadah*, Vanessa Ochs
The Song of Songs, Ilana Pardes
The *Daode Jing*, James Robson
Rumi's *Masnavi*, Omid Safi

The Book of *Revelation*

A BIOGRAPHY

Timothy Beal

PRINCETON UNIVERSITY PRESS

Princeton and Oxford

Requests for permission to reproduce material from this work
should be sent to permissions@press.princeton.edu

Published by Princeton University Press
41 William Street, Princeton, New Jersey 08540
6 Oxford Street, Woodstock, Oxfordshire OX20 1TR

press.princeton.edu

Library of Congress Control Number: 2018945516
ISBN: 978-0-691-14583-9

British Library Cataloging-in-Publication Data is available

Jacket art: Stanley Spencer (1891–1959), *Angels of the Apocalypse*,
1949 (oil on canvas). 61 × 91.4 cm / Private Collection /
Photo © Christie's Images / Bridgeman Images

Editorial: Fred Appel and Thalia Leaf
Text and Jacket/Cover Design: Lorraine Doneker
Production: Erin Suydam
Publicity: Tayler Lord

This book has been composed in Garamond Premier Pro

Printed on acid-free paper. ∞

Printed in the United States of America

10 9 8 7 6 5 4 3 2 1

CONTENTS

A few months ago, my bank mailed me a new credit card with the latest chip technology and a new expiration date. I was just about to call and activate it when I noticed that it also had a new security code on the back: 666.

A little chill ran down my spine, followed by a nervous chuckle. I thought back to my conservative evangelical youth in the 1970s and 1980s, when my friends and I would sometimes let our imaginations run wild thinking about the "mark of the Beast"—the idea, inspired by passages from the biblical book of Revelation, that in the last days the world would be lured into worshiping a seductively charming but ultimately Satanic beast, who would force his subjects to take his mark, the number 666, on their foreheads or right hands (Revelation 13). No one would be able to buy or sell anything without the mark.

Scholars have argued about the original referent of the number 666 in Revelation. Perhaps, as many believe, it stood for the first-century Roman Emperor Nero, whose name in Hebrew has the numerical value of 666. As a teenager, I had no such historical-critical insight. In my world, fraught with anxieties about the rise of computers and international banking, the number 666 was believed by many of my fellow Christians to be the mark of an emerging diabolical "one world government" that would wage war against the faithful. As a cashless society of credit cards and ATMs dawned, with one's identity and value increasingly tied to inscrutable financial numerologies disseminated across global networks, many of us end-times–minded Christians wondered whether we were witnessing the emergence of the very means by which the beast and his new world order would ascend to power.

Mary Stewart Relfe's best-selling 1981 book, *When Your Money Fails: The "666 System" Is Here*, gave expression to such apocalyptic anxieties. Among hundreds of signs of the "sudden world usage" of 666, she includes the following portents:

- World Bank code number is "666."
- New credit cards in U.S. are now being assigned the prefix "666."
- Central computers for Sears, Belk, J.C. Penney and Montgomery Ward prefix transactions with "666" as necessitated by computer programs.
- Shoes made in European Common Market Countries have stamped on inside label "666."
- Visa is 6 6 6; Vi, *Roman* Numeral, is 6; the "zz" sound, Zeta, the 6th character in the *Greek* alphabet, is 6; a, *English*, is 6 [i.e., flip the lower case "a" horizontally and it looks like a "6"].
- IRS began to require the prefix "666" on some forms; for example, W-2P, disability is 666.3; death is 666.4, etc., as early as 1977.

- President Carter's new Secret Security Force patches have on them "666."
- Identification tags on all foreign made Japanese parts for the Caterpillar Company, Peoria, Illinois, contain the code "666."
- A "new improved" fertilizer, Scotty's "666."
- Metric rulers distributed in 1979 throughout the U.S. have in center the number "666."
- Some U.S. School Systems for Junior High students began using a 6-6-6 System (6 subjects, 6 week report periods, 6 reports per year)[1]

After documenting these and many other instances, Relfe reflects,

> The poignant question facing us is how long will it be before we in the United States and the world must use his [the Beast's] number "666" . . . with which to buy and sell? Prepare yourself! Hold on to your hat! This is no gimmick! We are already using it! . . . Ah, John [writer of Revelation], you were more than a fisherman. . . . You were in the Spirit who showed you things to come.[2]

Some readers may balk at such seemingly paranoid apocalyptic speculations from the dawn of the computer age; others will remember them only too well.

Of course, like most kids in Christian youth culture, then as now, my friends and I were not entirely preoccupied with this kind of end-times fervor. We were also smoking weed, listening to the Talking Heads, racing our parents' station wagons, watching Rocky and

Bullwinkle reruns, falling in and out of love, and generally not taking our futures too seriously. Still, ball of teenaged contradictions that I was, there were moments when nightmare visions of being left behind in a world abandoned by God and ruled by diabolical beasts qua celebrity-politicians made terrifying sense to me. The Cold War was heating up, nuclear weapons were proliferating, and the United States and the USSR were jockeying for control in the Middle East—including Iraq, which was once ancient Babylon, the name of God's ultimate archenemy in Revelation.

This charismatic beast who would force everyone to take its mark was also sometimes referred to as "the Antichrist," a Satanic false messiah predicted to arrive before the Second Coming of Christ to seduce the masses into following and worshipping him. In fact, as with the rapture—the idea that believers will be raptured (from Greek *arpazo*, "steal" or "carry away") up to heaven before the end-time tribulations begin—the book of Revelation never mentions the Antichrist. This idea comes from the New Testament letters of John (not the same John as the author of Revelation), who warns believers against "antichrists" who deny that Jesus is the messiah (1 John 2:18, 22; 2 John 1:7). Such denial is, John says, "the spirit of the antichrist, of which you have heard that it is coming; and now it is already in the world" (1 John 4:3). In later Christian thought, however, John's rather generic antichrist, as anyone who denies Christ, merges with the beast of Revelation to become a singular Antichrist who will come to deceive the world into thinking that *he* is Christ. The chronology of visions in Revelation suggests that the Antichrist's arrival will precede the Second Coming, when Christ will defeat him and his armies at a place called Armageddon (perhaps a reference to the ruins of the ancient city of Megiddo in modern-day Israel) before establishing a new heaven and earth.

Not that any of us had a clue about the complex genealogy of biblical end-times ideas like the rapture, the beast, his mark, or the Antichrist. This stuff was coming to us many times removed, from best-selling books about the immanent end of the world like the biggest nonfiction best seller of the 1970s, Hal Lindsey's *The Late, Great Planet Earth* (1970), from Christian end-times horror movies like the church basement blockbuster *A Thief in the Night* (1972/3), and from Christian rock songs like Larry Norman's hugely popular 1968 song, "I Wish We'd All Been Ready," whose chorus laments, "There's no time to change your mind. The Son has come, and you've been left behind."[3]

I had tried and failed to read the actual text of the biblical book of Revelation. Like many before me, I got lost in all the overwhelmingly graphic descriptions of bloody, incredibly destructive battles involving myriad angels, gods, and monsters, all of whom I assumed carried symbolic meanings that were beyond my powers of decryption. For me, as for so many others throughout its history, Revelation was not so much a book to be read and interpreted as a simultaneously fascinating and disturbing multimedia mythosphere, a dense constellation of images, stories, and story-shaped images that scattered, overlapped and formed confused patterns in my religious imagination.

It has been decades since I have run in those end-times–oriented, conservative Christian circles. In the progressive liberal communities in which I worship and teach these days, few would touch that apocalyptic end of the Christian Bible with a ten-foot pole. I do not blame them. If I were not writing this book, I, too, might steer clear of it.

On the other hand, I have to admit that a bit of that apocalyptic imagination still resides in me. Despite my well-reasoned distance from it and the religious world it represents, I still get it. Like many former conservative evangelicals and fundamentalists, I still feel its weight. It may seem ridiculous to those who do not share this background, but I still get a little freaked out by the whole end-of-the-world scenario of seductive Satanic powers ruling over masses blinded by military might and sedated by consumptive decadence. Then again, come to think of it, maybe that scenario *should* be freaking us out these days.

Thus, I felt the little chill when my global, too-big-to-fail bank sent me a credit card with the number 666 as its security code.

In fact, there is a name for this fear of the number 666: *hexakosioihexekontahexaphobia* (Greek *hexakosioi*, "six hundred," plus *hexekonta*, "sixty," plus *hex*, "six," plus *phobia*). This phobia is indeed prevalent in our Revelation-infused Western society. Consider these hexakosioihexekontahexaphobic cases:

- In 1988, Ronald and Nancy Reagan left the White House and purchased a $2.5 million ranch house in the Bel Air neighborhood of Los Angeles whose address was 666 St. Cloud Road. Before moving in, they had the address changed in city records to 668 on account of a "mutual concern" that it could be interpreted as a sign of association with Satan.[4]

- In 2006, many pregnant women with summer due dates expressed concern about giving birth on June 6, that is, the sixth day of the sixth month of 2006—06/06/06—for fear of bad omens or, worse, inadvertently giving birth to the Antichrist.[5]

- In 2013, a high school athlete in Lexington, Kentucky, forfeited the regional cross-country championship race because she had been assigned bib number 666. "I didn't want to risk my relationship with God," she told a reporter. "I told them to mark out my name because it makes me sick just thinking that my name is associated with that number."[6]

- In 2015, Republican United States Representative Joe Barton of Texas had the number of his bill repealing a ban on crude-oil exports changed from 666 to 702.[7]

And, yes, in 2017 when religious studies professor Timothy Beal received a new credit card with the number 666 as its security code, he cut it up and closed the account.

It might seem odd to preface a biography of Revelation with a story about my own hexakosioihexekonta-hexaphobia. I do so in part to flag one of the ways my biography overlaps with Revelation's. Every biography is in some sense autobiographical, the result of living with its subject. Mine is no exception.

I also start here because this kind of apocalyptic sprawl—from a cryptic verse about a beast's number, to the metric system as a Satanic plot, to doomsday dread about a one-world government planting chips in our bodies, and so on, and so on—is what the life of Revelation looks like. Bits and pieces of this biblical tradition detach from their larger story world and find their way into new apocalyptic imaginaries. This biography of Revelation, then, is the story of a life in fragments, which detach, break up, scatter, recollect, attach, and reattach in often unexpectedly fascinating ways, ways that tend to be highly individual, even idiosyncratic.

In keeping with the titling conventions of its series, this book is called *The Book of Revelation: A Biography*. In this case, I invite readers to imagine the concept of *book* as broadly and loosely as possible. For this biography of Revelation is not the story of a singular life of a bound book of pages. Rather, it is a story of the many lives of an ever-expanding constellation of ideas and images that are more or less related to a first-century text tradition whose own origins are obscure and whose own status as Scripture has never been entirely secure.

Biographies are never comprehensive, but instead always selective. Biographers pick and choose moments they then turn into episodes that tell a story far more coherent and arc-shaped than any life can be. My selections are driven by an interest in attending to awakenings of new life for Revelation in a variety of cultural contexts and media environments. Thus, following the introduction and first chapter on the text's obscure origins, each chapter focuses on one particular cultural work, a particular instance of apocalypse that reveals and reincarnates Revelation on a new horizon of meaning.

There are a great many other fascinating lives of Revelation well worth attention. Among them: the place of Revelation in Christian missionary movements around the world, as well as within particular Protestant movements such as Pentecostalism, Jehovah's Witness, and Seventh Day Adventism; postcolonial interpretations and other uses of Revelation that subvert its Eurocentric or even Christocentric orientation in Western history; counterinterpretations to the prevalent anti-Catholic polemic among Protestants; Roman Catholic and Orthodox iconography; Revelation and the history of war, especially the American Civil War; images of heaven, resurrection, and the Last Judgment in Christian hymnology; and biblical rhetoric from Revelation in contemporary political discourses of the right and left. My hope is that the lives of Revelation to which I attend here are diverse and varied enough that readers will be inspired to explore others. I have tried to offer leads for such explorations in my suggestions for further reading at the end of this book.[8]

Above all, what I hope this biography reveals is Revelation's remarkable, shape-shifting, contagious vitality, for better and for worse, and with no end in sight.

The Book of *Revelation*

Introduction

The book of Revelation, located at the end of the New Testament, contains a series of dramatic apocalyptic visions that a man named John claims God reveals to him during his stay on Patmos, a small island off the west coast of Asia Minor (modern-day Turkey). Probably writing sometime between the beginning of the Jewish wars with Rome, which culminate in the destruction of the Jerusalem temple in 70 CE, and the end of the first century CE, this otherwise unknown John addresses his text to seven churches located on the nearby mainland. He exhorts them to persevere in their faithful obedience, describing wildly violent tribulations and a divine judgment that is soon to come, all of which will end in the annihilation of the present world. In its place, God will create a new heaven, a new earth, and a new Jerusalem where he and his Christ will reign with their angels and saints forever.

Also known as the Apocalypse of John (from the Greek *apokalupsis*, "from hiding" or "covering"), Revelation does not so much present a vision or prediction of the end of the world as it unveils the *edge* of the world. It is an ending that is also a beginning; it is an overwhelmingly violent, cosmopolitical end that is, in the same moment, an overwhelmingly extravagant new beginning in which death and suffering will be no more.[1] And all of it, all this shock and awe, is brought on as much by God, his Christ, and his angels as by God's monstrously diabolical enemies, the Satanic red dragon and his beasts. Dreadful and hopeful, dreamy and disgusting, Revelation is a sticky bit of biblical tradition: hard to grasp firmly and even harder to let go.

Indeed, no biblical book—perhaps no religious book—has been so simultaneously revered and reviled as Revelation. Many hail it as the pinnacle of prophetic vision and imagination, the cornerstone of the biblical canon, and, for those with eyes to see, the key to understanding the past, present, and future of the world and its creator. Others denounce it as downright diagnosable, the work of a highly disturbed individual whose highly disturbing dreams of inhumane and often misogynistic violence should never have been allowed into the Bible in the first place.

In fact, for as long as people have been reading this apocalyptic text, they have been arguing about its scriptural status and value. In the third century, Bishop Dionysius of Alexandria reported that many Christians reject it, "pronouncing it without sense and without reason . . . covered with such a dense and thick veil of ignorance." In his *Ecclesiastical History* (325 CE), Bishop Eusebius of Caesarea placed it in two mutually incompatible categories: as "undisputed" for some (that is, unquestionably belonging in the canon of Christian scriptures) and as "disputed" for others. And although Athanasius, Bishop of Alexandria, included it in his canonical list of New Testament scriptures in 367 CE, his contemporary, Cyril of Jerusalem, excluded it from his.

Over a millennium later, during the Reformation, the book of Revelation's status was still in question. In his 1522 edition of the New Testament, for example, Martin Luther wrote that he saw no evidence of its inspiration, that no one knows what it means, and that "there are many far better books for us to keep." Ironically, as we will see in chapter 6, Lucas Cranach the Elder's wildly creative woodcut illustrations of Revelation made it one of the most popular books in Luther's Bible.

Debates over the social and theological value of Revelation have chased it through history and continue to this day. Contemporary feminist biblical scholars, for example, disagree sharply as to its potential to contribute to social justice and liberation for women and nonheteronormative people. Some, notably Elisabeth Schüssler Fiorenza, argue that when its androcentric language is recognized as the "conventional, generic" rhetoric of its social-historical context, the narrative can proclaim a promise of liberation for poor and oppressed people regardless of gender and sexual identity. Others, notably Tina Pippin and Caroline Vander Stichele, argue that its gendered language of sexual violence is irredeemable insofar as it not only reflects but reinforces and ordains patriarchal norms and misogynistic representations of women.[2]

We will return to these debates about Revelation's scriptural status and value in subsequent chapters. For now, suffice it to say that, despite its great host of critics, the book of Revelation has not only survived, but thrived. Whether or not you have ever read the text, you are probably familiar with many of its scenes, characters, and images: the seven seals, the four horsemen, the red dragon, the "woman clothed in the sun," the archangel Michael, the "grapes of wrath," the "mark of the beast," the "whore of Babylon," the Second Coming, the thousand-year or millennial reign, the resurrection of the dead, the Last Judgment, the "book of life," the new Jerusalem, and so on. For better or worse, this book's extremely provocative visions have kindled the apocalyptic imaginations of so many artists, writers, leaders, and movements throughout history that it is virtually impossible for most people to imagine the world, or its end, without conjuring it.

Multimedia Constellation

Revelation begins in a place of displacement. "I was on the island of Patmos because of the word of God," its otherwise unknown author writes, "and I heard behind me a loud voice like a trumpet saying, 'Write in a book what you see'" (Revelation 1:10–11). That sense of being out of place, never quite at home, has never left it. Revelation is an outsider, a fringy, apocalyptic weirdo. Even when it finds itself welcomed into the palaces and temples of power and influence, as it often does, it remains a refugee and a stranger, an other within. As such, it never quite settles down. It continues to move, survive, and thrive by taking on different identities and adopting different forms in different times and places.

This biography of Revelation, then, is not about its life, but rather its many lives and the apocalyptic imaginations it has fueled. It explores the legion of often wildly contradictory lives of strangely familiar—sometimes horrifying, sometimes inspiring—biblical visions. It is the story of how Revelation continues to become something new, reinventing itself and taking on new forms of life in the hearts, minds, and imaginations of those who become its hosts.

My approach to this biography is that of a cultural historian. In the field of biblical studies, cultural history explores how biblical words, images, things, and ideas (including ideas of "the Bible") take particular meaningful forms in particular cultural contexts. A cultural-historical approach begins with the fact that there is no singular, fixed, original "Bible" or "book of the Bible" to be received across history. Rather, there are multiple, often competing, symbolic and material productions of the Bible—that is, biblical media—that are generated and generative in different cultural contexts.[3] In this light, the "book" of Revelation is not a self-evident, original literary thing created once and for all in the past and then incarnated in various interpretations throughout history. It constantly changes, forever being made and remade in different cultural productions of meaning.

This, then, is a "life" in and of fragments, bits and pieces, traces of traces of traces—often almost entirely detached from their "original" contexts—that keep mutating and replicating, congealing and dissolving into new cultural gene pools. Revelation is not so much a literary text, let alone a book to be received in later works, as it is a *multimedia constellation* of images, stories, and story-shaped images; it expands and contracts, with parts of it attaching to and detaching from other cultural artifacts within different media ecologies throughout history. It becomes part of different cultural works in unanticipated ways—ways that biblical scholars would often judge to be misuses, abuses, poor receptions, or no receptions at all.[4]

Very often, as we will see, this constellation becomes so diffuse and scattered that its elements detach altogether from anything like a "book." Unmoored from any kind of narrative whole, they circulate as snapshots that take on lives of their own, evolving, mutating, and reproducing in new contexts and combining with other cultural fragments of story and image.

Of course, floating somewhere near the dense middle of this multimedia constellation is a text, or rather a literary tradition, which, for the sake of convenience, we will call "the book of Revelation." This, too, is a constellation, an intertextual field whose boundaries and subfields are difficult, if not impossible, to map. There is no single "original" text of Revelation, but rather a large variety of manuscripts and bits of manuscripts—over three hundred, in fact—written in Greek, Latin, and other ancient languages and dated to the early centuries of Christianity. Biblical scholars sometimes call these various early manuscripts "witnesses" to a hypothetical original text. Whether such a singular original existed is a serious question. In any case, the oldest of these "witnesses" by far, Papyrus 98, a small fragment of papyrus scroll with nine verses from Revelation (1:13–2:1), dates to the second century CE. Even in its few surviving lines, its text does not entirely match later witnesses, including those that are primarily used to reconstruct the text of Revelation in most modern translations. Another early witness, Oxyrhynchus Papyrus 115, from the late third or early fourth century, gives the number of the beast in Revelation 13:18 as 616 rather than 666 (as do some other manuscripts).[5]

Surrounding this amalgamation of early manuscripts and manuscript fragments are the numerous critical scholarly editions and translations of Revelation. Some of these texts are translations of translations—early modern German and English translations from the Latin Vulgate ("common" or "popular") translation, for example. Others are translations of the so-called *textus receptus*, that is, the "received" whole Greek text of the New Testament that was used by Erasmus, Martin Luther, and the translators of the Geneva Bible and Authorized or "King James Version" Bible. Still others, including most modern translations like the New Revised Standard Version or the New International Version, are based on a reconstruction of what scholars hypothesize to have most likely been the "original" text based on critical assessment of the various "witnesses" to it. This text is known as the

Nestle-Aland *Novum Testamentum Graece*, which is now in its twenty-eighth revision.

These days, moreover, many versions and translations of Revelation proliferate well beyond traditional print book media, taking the form of everything from memes on social media like Instagram to huge online interfaces like Bible.com, which provides access to thousands of translations and encourages interaction with them via sharing in various social media.

We could go on, tracing the many paths of this literary constellation that we are short-handing as the "book" of Revelation: countless sermons, commentaries, interpretations, critical analyses, and so on. We could also look deeper into the middle of this literary mass and find the Jewish scriptural traditions that were worked and reworked into it. Indeed, much as John himself eats the scroll that the angel feeds him (Revelation 10:9–10), the text of Revelation itself is a voracious consumer of other texts. More than half of its verses are drawn from Jewish Scripture, especially prophetic texts like Ezekiel, Isaiah, and Daniel.

All that is to say, even when we try to narrow our focus to Revelation as a literary text, we find ourselves lost in a process of dissemination that calls into question the very notion that there is an original "book" behind it all. The closer we look, the more it seems to resist our desire for an origin, an *arche* to its literary expansions and contractions. To borrow from biblical media scholar Michael Hemenway, Revelation possesses a kind of *anarchic* textuality, a dynamism without beginning or end.[6]

Bolts in the Neck

In many respects, the multimedia constellation that we call Revelation is very like the popular cultural phenomenon that we call Frankenstein. First and most obviously, like Mary Shelley's *Frankenstein* (1818), Revelation is, at least in some sense, the monstrous creation of its writer, John of Patmos. Moreover, just as Shelley famously bid her "hideous progeny go forth and prosper" in the introduction of her 1831 republication of the novel, so John sent forth his own work into the world, where it has certainly prospered.

Yet John's text of Revelation is not only like Shelley's novel; it is also like the novel's monster, just as John is also like the monster's creator, Dr. Frankenstein. For, as we will see, the text of Revelation is not so much born from the mind of its creator as it is stitched together from pieces of other texts and then animated, given a life of its own.

Finally, like the Frankenstein phenomenon, Revelation is much more than its literary text. Just as many people know a lot about Frankenstein's monster without ever reading a word of the novel, so, too, many people know a lot about Revelation without ever having read a word of the biblical text.

What they know, moreover, often has little or nothing to do with that "original" text. How many think Frankenstein is the name of the monster, not its creator? How many believe he was brought to life by a lighteninggathering machine on a stormy night, when the novel describes no such dramatic scene? (Rather, Dr. Frankenstein very briefly recalls that he had a few medical instruments to "infuse a spark of being" while rain "pattered dismally" on the window pain.) Why do so many imagine the monster was hugely tall, with green skin and bolts sticking out of its neck, when no such features are described in the novel? And why do we imagine him dull and nearly mute, when Shelley's monster is exceptionally eloquent and deeply reflective about his existential predicament? Because the idea of Frankenstein is a multimedia cultural phenomenon that is far more than, and far different from, its "original" text. Like the monster itself, Frankenstein, as multimedia cultural phenomenon, has taken on a life—or rather many lives—of its own.

So, too, Revelation. How many think Revelation is where we learn about the Antichrist? Why do so many believe that Revelation claims believers will be taken up to heaven in the rapture? And why do so many believe it predicts the ultimate end of the world, when its final vision is of a renewed world—a new heaven and earth with a new Jerusalem? Because Revelation, too, is a multimedia cultural phenomenon that is far more than, and far different from, its "original" text tradition. The rapture and the Antichrist are like the bolts in the monster's neck.

Reading Notes

And yet, one might justifiably point out, there it is at the end of the Christian Bible: Revelation, a text of about twelve thousand words, divided into twenty-two chapters and 404 verses. Fair enough. It is as good a place to dive in as any.

If you have never read the book of Revelation, you are not alone. Many try but very few, Bible thumpers and Bible bashers alike, actually make it all the way through. Not because it has too many three-dollar words or difficult theological concepts. On the contrary, what drives the text is action: scenes of angels, gods, and monsters doing things, mostly violently ruinous things, to the earth and its human population, largely without any interpretation or explanation. Moreover, the main actors—the enthroned God, the image of the risen Christ as "the Lamb," the red dragon "who is the Devil and Satan," the beast, the beast's deputy prophet, and the hosts of angels breaking seals, blowing trumpets, and pouring out bowls of wrath—seem to spring from John's head out of nowhere, with little or no precedent in the rest of the New Testament. They simply do not seem like good "Bible." In actions and in appearance, they do not match what most consider the biblical ideas of God, Jesus, angels, Satan, the Gospel, and how all of them relate to humans and the rest of the world. Thus, the experience of reading Revelation does not jibe with what most expect from the Christian Bible.

Granted, it is easy enough to outline this biblical book. Most commentaries break it down something like this:

I. Introduction and opening vision of "one like the Son of Man" (Revelation 1:1–20)

Looking at it in this big-picture way, it appears sensible enough. However, when we start actually reading it, from one word to the next, most of us quickly lose sight of the forest for the trees. If you have thirty minutes to spare, I suggest you try reading it before continuing to read this. Whether or not you do that, what follows is my best attempt at an abridged overview.

> The revelation [*apokalupsis*] of Jesus Christ, which God gave him to show his servants [*doulois*, "slaves"] what must soon take place; he made it known by sending his angel to his servant John, who testified to the word of God and to the testimony of Jesus Christ, even to all that he saw. Blessed is the one who reads aloud the words of the prophecy, and blessed are those who hear and who keep what is written in it; for the time is near. (1:1–3; New Revised Standard Version translation)[7]

So John begins, boldly introducing his text as a revelation, in Greek an *apokalupsis*, literally an "uncovering" or "unveiling," from God to Jesus Christ to his angel to John.[8]

While on the island of Patmos "for the Word of the Lord and for the testimony of Jesus Christ" (in exile? by whom? in hiding? from whom? evangelizing? to whom?), John writes that he "was in the Spirit on the Lord's day" (probably Sunday, the first day of the week, when Jesus was believed to have been resurrected) when he heard the voice of a trumpet command him to write down what he sees in a scroll and to send it to the seven churches in Asia (1:9–11).[9]

When he turns to see whose voice it is, "I saw one like the Son of Man" in the midst of seven lampstands holding seven stars in his right hand.[10] He wears a white robe with a gold sash (Greek *zonē*, "girdle") across his chest (*mastois*, "breasts"), and his head and hair are white as wool, or snow. His eyes are fire, his feet are burnished bronze, and his voice is like many waters. His face shines like the sun. A double-edged sword protrudes from his mouth (1:12–16).

John collapses at his feet as if dead, but the terrifying figure touches John and says not to fear, revealing himself as the risen Christ. He tells John to write seven letters, one to each of the seven churches of Asia (Ephesus, Smyrna, Pergamum, Thyatira, Sardis, Philadelphia, and Laodicea, all in modern-day western Turkey).

The text then proceeds straight into Christ's dictation of the letters themselves, each introduced by "To the angel of the church of . . ." and then offering praise, criticism, or encouragement as the situation demands. Reading them now feels a little like listening in on one end of a phone call. Sometimes the issue is fairly clear, as when he criticizes a church for assimilating to mainstream Roman civil religion. Other times he focuses on now unknown persons or movements that he decries as antithetical to the faith: "the doctrine of Balaam," "the synagogue of Satan," the "Nikolaitans," and "that woman Jezebel" whom some are apparently tolerating or embracing.[11]

Already here, we see misogyny emerging, as Christ declares to the church of Thyatira,

> You tolerate that woman Jezebel, who calls herself a prophet and is teaching and beguiling my servants to practice fornication and to eat food sacrificed to idols. I gave her time to repent, but she refuses to repent of her fornication. Beware, I am throwing her on a bed, and those who commit adultery with her I am throwing into great distress, unless they repent of her doings; and I will strike her children dead. (2:20–23)

Here, someone who claims religious authority over John is represented as a woman who seduces others into illicit sex and religious syncretism. Her sexualized crime, John's Christ declares, calls for a perversely sexualized punishment: repeated rape and the murder of her offspring.[12]

After the seventh and final letter, John is immediately taken up "in the spirit" into heaven, and soon we find ourselves rushing with him from one extravagant vision to the next, usually introduced with a simple transitional phrase like "and I saw" or "and I heard." In heaven, John beholds a throne on a sea of glass with "one who looks like jasper and carnelian sitting in it." In front of it is a sea of glass, and above it is "a rainbow that looks like a giant emerald." Surrounding it are twenty-four more thrones with elders wearing golden crowns and white robes, as well as four six-winged "living creatures" or "animals" (Greek *zoa*), each "full of eyes all around and inside," front and back. One looks like a lion, one like an ox, one like an animal with a human face, and one like an eagle. Together these four creatures sing continually, "Holy, holy, holy, the Lord God the Almighty, who was and is and is to come." Every time they sing these lines, the twenty-four elders fall on their faces before the central throne, throwing their crowns down before the one seated there, singing their own praise song (4:1–11).

The text continues, "And I saw," just to the left of the main throne, a scroll with writing on both sides and sealed with seven seals. A great angel shouts, "Who is worthy to open the scroll and break its seals?" (5:2). When John realizes that no one, in heaven or on earth, is able to open it, he weeps bitterly, but one of the twenty-four elders comforts him, saying that the conquering Lion of Judah, descendant of King David, can do it.

At this point "a Lamb standing as if slaughtered, having seven horns and seven eyes" (5:6), steps forth from between the throne and the elders. He takes the scroll from the hand of the one seated on the throne. The elders, holding harps and bowls of incense, begin singing praises to the Lamb:

> You are worthy to take the scroll and to open its seals,
> for you were slaughtered and by your blood you ran-
> somed for God saints from every tribe and language

and people and nation; you have made them to be a kingdom and priests serving our God, and they will reign on earth. (5:9–10)

"And I saw and I heard" thousands and thousands of angels around the living creatures and the elders also singing, along with all creatures in heaven, on earth, under the earth, and in the sea.

John continues, "And I saw" the Lamb open the scroll, one seal at a time, each followed by one of the creatures calling forth another portent. The first four seals unleash ominous horses and riders: first, a white horse whose rider carries a bow and wears a crown to conquer; second, a bright red horse whose rider wields a huge sword to steal peace from the earth so that people will slaughter one another; third, a black horse whose rider holds a pair of scales; and fourth, a pale green horse whose rider, named Death, is followed by Hades. These latter two bring death by sword, famine, pestilence, and wild animals.

When the Lamb opens the fifth seal, the souls of those "slaughtered for the word of God" (6:9) suddenly cry out from under an altar, asking God how long it will be before he will avenge their deaths. They are given white robes and told to wait a little longer.

When the sixth seal is opened, the earth quakes, the sun goes black, the moon turns blood-red, the stars fall from the sky like fruit from a tree, and the sky rolls up like a giant scroll. Terrified, all the earth's inhabitants, from kings and generals to slaves, hide in caves and crags, begging the rocks of the mountains to fall on them to hide them from the Lamb's wrath.

"After this I saw" four angels with the power to destroy the earth and sea. They hold the four corners of earth and are just about to shake it out like a dirty rug, when another angel comes down from the rising sun and forbids them from doing so until the 144,000 servants of God, 12,000 from each of the twelve tribes of Israel, have been sealed on their foreheads. Then multitudes of people from every tribe and nation, all dressed in robes washed white with the blood of the Lamb, gather before the throne and the Lamb, singing praises. Thousands upon thousands of angels, the twenty-four elders, and the four living creatures fall on their faces before the throne, singing more praises.

Then the Lamb opens the seventh and final seal, and there is silence in heaven "for about half an hour," followed by John's testimony: "And I saw" seven angels before the throne who were given trumpets. And another angel takes an incense bowl, fills it with fire and incense, offers it before the throne, and pours it out on the earth, which shakes with thunder and lightning and earthquakes.

Thus begins another sequence of seven portents, each inaugurated by an angel blowing a trumpet. First, hail and fire mixed with blood is poured on the earth, burning up one third of the land, one third of the trees, and one third of the green grass. Second, a mountain engulfed in flames is hurled into the sea, so that one third of the sea becomes blood, one third of all sea creatures are killed, and one third of all ships are destroyed. Third, a star named Wormwood falls on one third of the rivers and springs, and one third of the waters become wormwood, poisoning many. Fourth, one third of the sun, moon, and stars are darkened, taking light away from both day and night.

At this point things begin to ramp up. When the fifth angel blows the fifth trumpet, a star descends from heaven to earth and is given the key to the shaft of the bottomless pit. When he opens it, there emerge swarms of locusts with human faces, women's hair, scales like iron breastplates, lion's teeth, and scorpion's tales. They wear golden crowns and armor like war horses, and "in their tails is their power to harm people for five months." Their king is the ruling angel of the bottomless pit, whose Hebrew name is Abaddon ("destruction" or "ruin," from the verb *'abad*). They were told not to hurt the grass or green plants but to torture any humans who do not have the seal of God on their foreheads.

The sixth trumpet signals the release of four angels from the river Euphrates. They lead 200 million cavalry with sulfur-breathing horses that have heads of lions and tails of serpents and riders with breastplates of fire, and they go forth to slaughter one third of all humankind.

Before the seventh trumpet can sound, another angel appears. Wrapped in clouds, with a rainbow above his head, his face is like the sun, and he has legs like pillars of fire. He holds a small scroll open in his hand. With one foot on the land and one on the sea, he shouts, and seven thunders reply. John is about to write down what the thunders say when the angel forbids him to do so, explaining,

"In the days when the seventh angel is to blow his trumpet, the mystery of God will be fulfilled."

The trumpet voice from heaven then tells John to take the little scroll from the giant angel and, when he does, the angel tells him to eat it, which he does. It tastes as sweet as honey but makes him sick to his stomach. Both the trumpet voice and the angel tell him to prophesy and also to take a measuring rod and measure the temple of God, its altar, and the people who worship there—but not to measure its courtyard, because it has been given over to foreign nations, who will trample Jerusalem for forty-two months.

At this point, things get a little confusing. An unidentified voice declares that "I" will give "my two witnesses" (*martursin*, "martyrs" or "witnesses") the authority to prophesy for 1,260 days and that they are the two olive trees and lampstands, mentioned for the first time here, that stand before the Lord (11:3). They will have the power to shut up the sky, turn water to blood, and start plagues at will, and anyone who tries to harm them while they are prophesying will be consumed by fire from their mouths. When the two witnesses have finished their prophesying, the beast of the bottomless pit will rise up and kill them. Their bodies will lie rotting in the street, and the people against whom they had prophesied will glare and gloat, celebrate and exchange gifts.

Switching from future to past tense, the voice goes on to say that, after three and a half days, the breath of life from God entered their corpses. They stood up and rose to heaven in a cloud as the masses watched in dreaded amazement. Then an earthquake destroyed one tenth of the city and killed seven thousand people. The survivors gave glory to God.

Finally, the seventh angel blows its trumpet. Immediately, loud voices in heaven declare, "The kingdom of the world has become the kingdom of our Lord and of his Messiah, and he will reign forever and ever" (11:15). The twenty-four elders fall on their faces, singing praises and thanksgivings for God's Last Judgment, and God's temple in heaven is opened. Amid thunder, lightning, earthquakes, and hail, John sees the Ark of the Covenant inside the temple.

Whether what follows is a continuation of the same scene in heaven or a new scene is unclear. In any case, John sees a "great portent" in heaven: a woman in labor, clothed with the sun, with the moon beneath her feet and a crown of twelve stars. She is crying out in birthing pangs. This is followed by another portent: a great seven-headed, ten-horned red dragon, his tail sweeping down a third of the stars in heaven as he waits before the woman in order to eat the baby, who is to rule the world, the moment it is born. But the baby is immediately snatched up to God in heaven, and the woman flees to the wilderness where God has prepared a place for her to wait for 1,260 days (the same amount of time that the two witnesses are to prophesy before being killed by the beast of the bottomless pit).

Then a war erupts in heaven between the archangel Michael and his angels on the one hand and the dragon, "that ancient serpent, who is called the Devil and Satan," and his angels on the other. Michael's forces are victorious, as the devil dragon and his angels are thrown down to earth, where he chases the woman clothed in the sun, who is given wings to fly to the wilderness. From his mouth, the dragon spews a raging river of water to sweep her away, but Earth (Greek *Gaia*) comes to her rescue, swallowing the flood. Enraged, the dragon leaves the woman in the wilderness and instead attacks her children, who are the righteous ones of God.

As the dragon takes a stand on the seashore, John sees a beast rise out of the sea. It has ten horns and seven crowned heads, with each head bearing a blasphemous name. One of its heads has been healed from a mortal wound. It is like a leopard with bear's feet and a lion's mouth, and it curses and blasphemes God and all who dwell in heaven. The dragon gives the beast authority, and the whole earth worships it for forty-two months.

John continues, "And I saw" another beast, this one rising out of the earth, with two Lamb's horns and a dragon's voice. This beast acts as deputy, deceiving everyone into worshiping the first beast by performing signs and miracles. It creates an image of the first beast, gives it breath, and allows it to speak, killing anyone who does not worship it. It is in this context that John introduces the number 666:

> Also it causes all, both small and great, both rich and poor, both free and slave, to be marked on the right hand or the forehead, so that no one can buy or sell who does not have the mark, that is, the name of the

beast or the number of its name. This calls for wisdom: let anyone with understanding calculate the number of the beast, for it is the number of a person. Its number is six hundred sixty-six. (13:16–18)

"And I saw" the Lamb, standing on Mount Zion accompanied by 144,000 righteous men, all virgins who have not "defiled themselves with a woman" and have never lied, bearing the names of the Lamb and God on their foreheads. At the same time, John hears a voice in heaven like the sound of many waters, of thunder, and of harps singing a new song before the throne, the four animals, and the twenty-four elders, but no one except the 144,000 can learn the song.

Three angels then appear in mid-heaven, each making a proclamation: the first carries an "eternal Gospel" and calls all to fear God, for judgment is coming; the second proclaims, "Fallen, fallen is Babylon the great! She has made all nations drink of the wine of the wrath of her fornication" (14:8); and the third declares that all who worship the beast and its image will drink the undiluted wine of God's wrath through relentless torment with fire and sulfur so that the smoke of their endless suffering will rise forever.

"And I saw" a white cloud with one like the Son of Man sitting on it, wearing a golden crown and holding a sharp sickle. An angel comes out of the temple and tells him to reap, because it is harvest time for the earth. So he swings his sickle across the earth. Then another angel comes out of the temple, and he too holds a sickle. He is followed by yet another, who has authority over fire, and who tells the sickle-wielding angel to use his sickle to gather the grape clusters of the earth, because they are ripe. That angel does so and throws the vintage of the earth into the "great wine press of the wrath of God." The wine press is trampled outside the city, and the blood flows, high as a horse's bridle, for two hundred miles.

Seven angels dressed in bright robes with gold sashes come out of the temple in heaven, and the four creatures give each one of them a bowl of divine wrath in the form of a plague. The first pours his bowl on the earth, and it causes painful sores on those who have taken the mark of the beast and worshiped him. The second pours his bowl on the sea, and it becomes like the blood of a corpse; everything in it dies. The third pours his into the rivers, and they become as blood. The fourth pours his on the sun, and it scorches the people of the earth, yet they still refuse to repent. The fifth pours his on the beast's throne so that his kingdom is cast into darkness, yet the people do not repent, even as they gnaw their own tongues off and curse God in agony. The sixth pours his bowl on the river Euphrates, and it dries up to prepare the way of the kings from the East.

Then, before the seventh angel can pour his bowl, four spirits come out of the mouths of the dragon, the beast, and his false prophet, who station them for battle at the place called Armageddon. The seventh angel then pours his bowl into the air, and a voice declares, "It is finished," as lightning flashes, thunder booms, and the earth shakes. The great city is split into three parts, the islands and mountains run away and hide, and hundred-pound hail-stones crush the population, which continues to curse God in their misery.

At this point, one of the angels carries John into the wilderness to see the judgment on the "great whore" of Babylon, "with whom the kings of the earth have committed fornication, and with the wine of whose fornication the inhabitants of the earth have become drunk" (17:2). Adorned in purple and scarlet and fine jewels, riding a scarlet beast with seven heads and ten horns above many waters, she holds a golden cup of abominations and impurities, and is drunk on the blood of saints and witnesses to Jesus. On her forehead is written, "Babylon the great, mother of whores and of earth's abominations" (17:5). As John stands in stunned amazement, the angel explains to him the mysteries of the woman and the beast:

> "The beast that you saw was, and is not, and is about to ascend from the bottomless pit and go to destruction. And the inhabitants of the earth, whose names have not been written in the book of life from the foundation of the world, will be amazed when they see the beast, because it was and is not and is to come.
>
> "This calls for a mind that has wisdom: the seven heads are seven mountains on which the woman is seated; also, they are seven kings, of whom five have fallen, one is living, and the other has not yet come; and when he comes, he must remain only a little while. As for the beast that was and is not, it is an eighth but it belongs to the seven, and it goes to

destruction. And the ten horns that you saw are ten kings who have not yet received a kingdom, but they are to receive authority as kings for one hour, together with the beast. These are united in yielding their power and authority to the beast; they will make war on the Lamb, and the Lamb will conquer them, for he is Lord of lords and King of kings, and those with him are called and chosen and faithful."

And he said to me, "The waters that you saw, where the whore is seated, are peoples and multitudes and nations and languages. And the ten horns that you saw, they and the beast will hate the whore; they will make her desolate and naked; they will devour her flesh and burn her up with fire. For God has put it into their hearts to carry out his purpose by agreeing to give their kingdom to the beast, until the words of God will be fulfilled. The woman you saw is the great city that rules over the kings of the earth." (17:8–18)

With that mystery cleared up, John turns to see another angel, bright with splendor, proclaiming in song (much of it drawn from the Hebrew biblical prophets) the downfall of Babylon, still personified as the "great whore," as the kings and merchants of the earth who followed after and fornicated with her cry out in lamentation over her violent end.

After this the voice of a great multitude in heaven, and the voice of the twenty-four elders and the four living creatures, the voice of the throne, and finally the voice with the sound of many waters and thunder peals, sing hallelujahs to God, declaring that the time of the marriage of the Lamb has come, and his bride is ready. The angel says to John, "Write this: Blessed are those who are invited to the marriage supper of the Lamb" (19:9). John bows down to worship the angel, and the angel reprimands him, saying that he should only worship God.

As heaven opens, John sees a white horse whose crowned rider, Christ, leads all the armies of heaven. He has eyes like fire and wears a robe dipped in blood. A sword comes forth from his mouth to smite the nations, whom he will rule with an iron rod. His name is "Faithful and True," and he has a name inscribed that no one knows but himself. He is named "the Word of God," and on his robe and thigh is inscribed the name "King of kings and Lord of lords" (19:11–16). Another angel, standing in the sun, commands all the birds of mid-heaven to gather for the "great supper of God," feasting on the flesh of the warriors, captains, horses, and riders—free and slave, great and small alike—as the beast and the kings of the earth make war against the crowned horseman and the armies of heaven.

Finally, the beast is captured, along with his deputy beast, and they are thrown into the lake of fire. The rest are slain by the sword coming from the mouth of Christ, and the birds sate themselves on the flesh of the fallen.

John continues describing his vision: "And I saw" another angel, holding a chain and a key to the bottomless pit, who seizes the dragon, "that ancient serpent, who is the Devil and Satan," and locks him up for a thousand years. After that time, John says, he will be released for a little while. "And I saw" those seated on thrones given authority to judge, and all the souls of those beheaded for the sake of Jesus and the word of God come back to life and reign as priests with Christ for a thousand years. John calls this the "first resurrection" and says that the rest of the dead will not be resurrected until after the thousand-year reign. At that time, he continues, Satan will be released and will be allowed to deceive the nations once again. He will gather armies "at the four corners of the earth, Gog and Magog" (20:8).

Then the great army surrounds the camp of the saints in the holy city, preparing to annihilate them, but fire comes down from heaven and swallows them up. Their leader, the devil dragon, is thrown into the lake of fire where he joins the beast and his false prophet in eternal torture and torment. "And I saw" the great white throne and the one seated upon it, and the whole earth flees from his presence. "And I saw" all the dead come back to life. The sea gives up its dead, and so do Death and Hades, after which they, too, are thrown into the lake of fire. John explains that this is "the second death." The newly raised dead are gathered before the throne and are judged according to their works. Anyone whose name is found in "the book of life" is also thrown into the lake of fire.

With the former earth and sea now passed away, John proclaims, "I saw a new heaven and a new earth" with the holy city of Jerusalem coming down from heaven "like a bride adorned for her husband" (21:1–2). "And I heard" the voice from the throne declare,

> See, the home of God is among mortals.
> He will dwell with them as their God;
> they will be his peoples,
> and God himself will be with them;
> he will wipe every tear from their eyes.
> Death will be no more;
> mourning and crying and pain will be no more,
> for the first things have passed away. (21:3–4)

This voice continues speaking to John, telling him that he makes all things new, that he is "the Alpha and the Omega," that he will quench the thirsty with the water of life and they will be his children. "But as for the cowardly, the faithless, the polluted, the murderers, the fornicators, the sorcerers, the idolaters, and all liars, their place will be in the lake that burns with fire and sulfur, which is the second death" (21:8).

Then one of the angels who poured out one of the bowls of wrath shows John the bride betrothed to the Lamb, that is, the new Jerusalem. John writes that she bears divine radiance and looks like a gigantic rare gem of jasper or crystal. Its (Her?) high walls have twelve gates, each one a giant pearl that bears one of the names of the twelve tribes of Israel, and twelve foundations, each adorned with jewels and bearing of the names of the twelve disciples of Jesus. The angel measures the city with a golden rod. It is a perfect cube, measuring 1,500 miles deep, 1,500 miles wide, and 1,500 miles high, and its wall measures 144 cubits (over two hundred feet). The wall is made of jasper and the city of pure gold.

"And I saw" no temple in the new city, "for its temple is the Lord God the Almighty and the Lamb." Nor is there sun or moon, for God is its sun, and the Lamb is its moon. There will never be night, the gates will never be shut, and all the kings and nations of the earth will bring their glory and honor into it. Yet, John adds, nothing unclean and no one who practices abominations or lies will be permitted to enter it—only those whose names are in the book of life.

The angel also shows him "the river of the water of life," which flows from the thrones of God and of the Lamb. It runs down the street in the middle of the city, and the tree of life grows on either side of it, producing twelve fruits and leaves that will be used to heal the nations. The righteous will worship God and the Lamb, face to face, wearing his name on their foreheads.

Then he (the angel? God? the Lamb? At this point it is more difficult than ever to know who is speaking) tells John that all John has seen and heard is true, that he is coming soon, and that anyone who keeps the words of the prophecy of this book, which John has written, will be blessed. John once again falls before the angel to worship him, and the angel once again reprimands him, promising judgment to come that will include blessings for the righteous and eternal torment for evildoers.

Jesus confirms everything: "It is I, Jesus, who sent my angel to you with this testimony for the churches. I am the root and the descendant of David, the bright morning star" (22:16). Then he (still Jesus? John?) offers a warning that if anyone adds to the words of the prophecy of this book, the plagues described herein will be heaped upon them, and if anyone removes anything from this book, their names will be removed from the book of life.

Finally, "The one who testifies to these things says, 'Surely I am coming soon.' Amen. Come, Lord Jesus! The grace of the Lord Jesus be with all the saints. Amen" (22:20–21).

Generative Incomprehensibility

So ends John's Revelation, or rather his barrage of revelations, scenes of fantastic violence and brilliant extravagances, piled one on top of another without pause or transition except "and I saw" or "and I heard."

It is indeed an overwhelming experience to read all at once, even in the abridged form I have offered here. The first time I taught a college course on Revelation, I had my students read the entire book on their own in preparation for our discussion. That turned out to be a mistake. One student was so traumatized by the experience that she did not return to class for over a week in hopes of avoiding any further encounter with the text. Another fell asleep while reading it on the beach and awoke an hour later in the middle of a violent thunderstorm, fearing that John's vision of divine wrath was coming true.

These days when I teach Revelation, we start by reading it out loud, together, in class. That, too, is an overwhelming, even exhausting experience, but sharing it helps maintain some critical distance.

When we are finished, I will often ask students to get out a piece of scratch paper and try to draw one of its wilder scenes—the first vision of "one like the Son of Man," for example, or the four many-winged creatures "with eyes all around and inside," or the twenty-four elders repeatedly bowing and throwing down their crowns before the throne *and* singing a new song to the victorious Lamb, who stands "as if slaughtered," *and* talking to John about the scroll while the four creatures sing.

These literary images remind us that texts can do things that pictures cannot, and vice versa. They are written descriptions that defy visual depiction. Time and space unfold in John's descriptions of his visions in ways that, paradoxically, simply cannot be translated into visual images. As such, John's literary images simultaneously provoke and resist our capacities of reason and imagination, eliciting what Maia Kotrosits aptly calls "affective hyper-saturation," a volatile mix of feelings and resonances that resist any singular interpretation or representation and instead invite readers and hearers into "impressionistic imagination."[13]

It is this *generative incomprehensibility*, I suggest, that is key to the many lives of Revelation. It is a revelation, an uncovering, of things that remain hidden, a seeing of things that remain unseeable. They simultaneously demand and refuse visualization. They cannot stay put on the page but inevitably spill over into other media, morphing as they attach to other narratives and apocalyptic imaginaries quite foreign to John's own.

Pale Rider

Obscure Origins

CHAPTER 2

> I, John, your brother who share with you in Jesus
> the persecution and the kingdom and the patient
> endurance, was on the island called Patmos because
> of the word of God and the testimony of Jesus.
>   —*Revelation 1:9*

"Well, who's that a writin'?" asked gospel singer and blues legend Blind Willie Johnson in his 1930 song, "John the Revelator." Who *is* this? *What* is this? "Ask the Revelator," Johnson offers. But John the Revelator is lost to us, save his text. And his text does not readily yield answers.

To borrow back an image that Hollywood borrowed from John's vision of the fourth horseman of the Apocalypse, the text of Revelation seems to have entered the scene of early Christianity like the darkly religious stranger called Preacher in Clint Eastwood's blockbuster Western, *Pale Rider*. He rides into town, seemingly out of nowhere, hell following after him, his religious identity and history of violence veiled yet unmistakable.

Soon people are talking: Who was this John of Patmos, as we have come to call him? Where and when did he come from?

The intense fervor of his faith in God's Christ, his virulent hatred for those who would compromise that faith, even in the face of state-sanctioned torture and death, and his propensity for graphic descriptions of cosmic destruction and mass bloodshed suggest that he is no stranger to the sharp, pointy end of the *Pax Romana*, or "peace of Rome," which was maintained with an iron hand in provinces like Judea and its holy city, Jerusalem, the political and symbolic center of Jewish identity.

Some say John wrote his Revelation during or shortly after the first Jewish war against Rome, remembered as the "Great Revolt," which lasted from 66 to 70 CE and ended with the decimation of Jerusalem and the total destruction of its temple.[1] Rome had occupied Judea since 63 BCE, and before that had controlled the area by means of procurators who taxed the Judean people and delivered taxes to the emperor according to quotas. Throughout the first half of the first century CE, especially during the reign of Emperor Caligula (37–41 CE), who enforced an unprecedented imperial cult devoted to himself as a living god, tensions between Rome and the Jewish people had been escalating in Judea and throughout the empire.

In 40 CE, for example, the Jewish philosopher Philo led a delegation of Jewish leaders from Egypt to Rome after Greek mobs sacked their neighborhoods and forced survivors to eat pork in honor of Caligula's birthday.[2] Philo describes mobs stoning Jews in the streets, burning whole Jewish families alive, and dragging others to death behind horses, all the while mocking their victims like actors in a theater troupe.[3]

At the same time, Judea had become something of a powder keg, with increasing protests against Rome's tax policies and a growing movement of radical revolutionary zealots seeking religious liberty and an independent Judean state by whatever means necessary. According to the Jewish historian Josephus, these tensions were ignited into an all-out conflict when a Greek merchant in Caesarea set an earthen vessel upside down in the entrance of the synagogue and began sacrificing birds on it. "This thing," Josephus writes,

> provoked the Jews to an incurable degree, because their laws were affronted, and the place was polluted. Whereupon the sober and moderate part of the Jews thought it proper to have recourse to their governors again, while the seditious part, and such as were in the fervor of their youth, were vehemently inflamed to fight. The seditions also among the Gentiles of Cesarea stood ready for the same purpose; for they had, by agreement, sent the man to sacrifice beforehand so that it soon came to blows.[4]

On hearing this, Gessius Florus, the Roman procurator of Judea, sent men to Jerusalem and set up a tribunal to discover who was inciting disrespect among the Jews. When no culprits emerged by that means, Florus sent soldiers into the marketplace to slaughter anyone they found. According to Josephus, they killed 3,600 men, women, children, and babies.[5] He continued his crackdown another day before returning to Rome, leaving the city in turmoil.

Herod Agrippa II, the king of Judea at the time, tried to quell the unrest, encouraging everyone simply to wait out Florus, who would soon be replaced as procurator anyway. But this recommendation angered those already inclined to rebellion. They drove him and his sister, Bernice, out of the city. They took the hilltop city of Masada, killing the Romans who lived there, and ordered the high priest of the Jerusalem temple to cease offering sacrifices for Caesar.

The rebels soon took control of Jerusalem, killing those who sided with Agrippa in supporting a peaceful solution. They burned down the palaces of the king and Bernice as well as the house of the high priest. They also burned up the contracts of creditors, thereby winning the hearts of the poor and, ultimately, as Josephus put it, "burnt down the nerves of the city."[6] At this point, the Jewish rebellion quickly escalated into full-scale war against Rome as the legate of Syria sent tens of thousands of troops to northern Judea, pressing toward Jerusalem. The rebels ultimately pushed them back, however, killing thousands before the legate escaped back home to Damascus.

In 67 CE, General, soon-to-be Emperor, Vespasian, with his son Titus as second-in-command, attacked the Jewish rebels in Galilee with assistance from King Agrippa II's armies. They soon had control of most of Judea, leaving the rebel stronghold of Jerusalem to weaken itself with in-fighting among its different factions. Civil conflicts elsewhere in the empire distracted Rome from finishing the job until 70 CE, when now Emperor Vespasian sent Titus back to take Jerusalem. After a devastating seven-month siege, his legion broke through the city's last defenses, sent its last fighters into retreat, and destroyed its temple. Well over a century later, the Roman historian Cassius Dio offers this poignant account of the culminating desecration:

> The entrance to the temple was now laid open to the Romans. The soldiers on account of their superstition would not immediately rush in, but at last, as Titus forced them, they made their way inside. Then the Jews carried on a defence much more vigorous than before, as if they had discovered a rare and unexpected privilege in falling near the temple, while fighting to save it. The populace was stationed in the outer court, the senators on the steps, and the priests in the hall of worship itself. And though they were but a handful fighting against a far superior force they were not subdued until a section of the temple was fired. Then they went to meet death willingly, some letting themselves be pierced by the swords of the Romans, some slaughtering one another, others committing suicide, and others leaping into the blaze.[7]

Titus then returned to Rome, leaving his legion to take out the few remaining Judean strongholds, the last one in 72 or 73 CE being the famous hilltop walled city of Masada. According to Josephus, whose account is our only surviving source, the city's rebel leader, Eleazar, compelled its inhabitants to commit collective suicide rather than surrender.

Here, then, was a crisis that called for new theological interpretations of Jewish history. It was, in many respects, as massive a crisis as the fall of Jerusalem, the destruction of the first temple, and the exile of its inhabitants by the Babylonians in 587 BCE. Indeed, these two destructions, both at the hands of imperial superpowers, are the primary shaping forces of Jewish and Christian scriptural memory.[8]

It is certainly conceivable that this war was the crucible of John's Revelation, in which Rome is the new Babylon, laying waste to the righteous ones, their holy city, Jerusalem, and their temple.

In the Shadow of Empire

Others say John's crucible was nearly two decades later, toward the end of the reign of Emperor Domitian (81–96 CE), who was remembered by later Christian tradition as a notoriously ruthless persecutor of Jews and Christians.

Domitian built an impressive cult of personality around himself, gaining popular acclaim and the respect of the military, but aggravating the aristocracy. After his assassination by court officials, the Senate condemned his memory to oblivion, melting down his coins, tearing down his arches, and erasing his name from public records. Roman historians such as Pliny the Younger took pains to disparage him as an egomaniacal tyrant, set in sharp contrast against his successors, especially Emperor Trajan (98–117 CE), who was celebrated as the greatest of all Roman emperors and praised by later Christians as a righteous pagan.[9]

More than two centuries later, after Christianity had become the official religion of the Roman Empire, Bishop Eusebius of Caesarea, in his *Ecclesiastical History* (about 325 CE), adopted this exceedingly critical view of Domitian, describing his "hatred and enmity toward God" expressed in aggressive persecutions of Christians and Jews, and quoting an earlier source saying that he had commanded that all descendants of David be slain because they were related genealogically to Christ. It was under his reign, Eusebius writes, that the John of Revelation was "condemned to dwell on the island of Patmos in consequence of his testimony to the divine word," quoting with approval Irenaeus, who says that "the one who saw the revelation" was writing "not long ago, but almost in our own generation, at the end of the reign of Domitian."[10]

Most lay persons today, along with many contemporary scholars, would likewise date John's Revelation to Domitian's reign. But that dating depends on something of a broken circular argument: first, that Revelation was probably written during a time of persecution against Christians and Jews; second, that Irenaeus, writing several decades later, says John's Revelation dates to the end of Domitian's reign; and third, that Domitian was remembered by anti-Domitian, pro-Trajan Roman historians and later Christians as a tyrant and an aggressive persecutor of Christians and Jews. The problem in this logic is that most who make this argument also acknowledge that historical research does not bear out this Christian memory of Domitian as especially monstrous or anti-Christian. There were no general statewide persecutions of Christians, Jews, or other religious minorities under Domitian, Nero, or any other emperor until much later, in the third century. Although certainly horrifying for those witnessing or suffering them, persecutions of Christians and Jews as resisters of Roman civil religion tended to be sporadic and individual. Thus, dating John to Domitian's reign means taking Irenaeus's word for it, even though, despite Eusebius's assertion otherwise, that period was not one of particularly infamous empire-wide religious persecution.[11]

Today, the remains of a gigantic temple dedicated to Domitian are strewn over a large open area on a high spot near the upper agora of Ephesus, a major Roman port city in Asia Minor and the location of one of the seven churches addressed in the book of Revelation (2:1–7). The temple had stood high above the city, built on a two-story platform about fifty meters wide and one hundred meters long. But now, only fragments remain: broken columns, building blocks, and the huge marble head, left forearm, and pieces of a leg from a seven-meter-tall statue of Domitian himself. Standing amidst these crumbled remains today, it is not hard to imagine the powerful presence that this temple, dedicated to the emperor, would have held in the city.

Indeed, if John of Patmos were writing toward the end of Domitian's reign, explicitly addressing the church at

Ephesus in one of the seven letters, why would he not have mentioned this temple? After all, he does allude to the Roman temple in the city of Pergamum, "where Satan's throne is" (2:13). In any case, whether written in the shadow of Domitian's temple or some other towering figure of Roman imperial religious power and might, John's Revelation certainly seems to be familiar with the shadow side of the *Pax Romana*.

Not *That* John

Most agree that this John, writing from Patmos, was not John the apostle, the beloved disciple of Jesus traditionally believed to be the writer of the Gospel of John and the three letters of John. No doubt being mistaken for that John helped promote this John's Revelation within the early Christian movement, eventually securing it a spot in the canon of Christian Scripture we call the New Testament. Justin Martyr, in his *Dialogue with Trypho* (c. 150 CE), a fictional argument with a Jew about the messianic identity of Jesus, states plainly, apparently without needing to argue the point, that the John of Revelation was John the apostle.[12] Likewise Irenaeus, writing a few decades later in *Against Heresies* (c. 170s or 180s CE), calls him "the Lord's disciple," describing him as the very one who leaned on Christ's bosom at the Last Supper.[13]

Other early Christian writers questioned this identification. Eusebius quotes the late first-century or early second-century Christian leader Papias who mentions two different Johns, the apostle John and John "the presbyter," both of whom he considered to be authoritative. Eusebius suggests that this second John is the John of Revelation, which would explain why it is said that there are two revered Johns buried in Ephesus, which is near Hierapolis where Papias served as bishop.[14]

Later in his history, Eusebius also quotes at length one Dionysius of Alexandria (mid-200s CE), who writes that many Christians of his time consider Revelation to be an ill-conceived fake that claims John as its author to gain credibility:

> Some before us have set aside and rejected the book altogether, criticising it chapter by chapter, and pronouncing it without sense or argument, and maintaining that the title is fraudulent. For they say that it is not the work of John, nor is it a revelation, because it is covered thickly and densely by a vail of obscurity. *ℓ* And they affirm that none of the apostles, and none of the saints, nor any one in the Church is its author.[15]

These critics, Dionysius says, believed the actual author was Cerinthus, who founded a sect that believed that the kingdom of God would be an earthly one and indulged in "eating and drinking and marrying, and in festivals and sacrifices and the slaying of victims." Cerinthus, they speculate, used the pseudonym of John to leverage authority for his text.

Dionysius does not believe that the book is pseudonymous, but rather that it was written by a different John. He goes on to compare this text with that of the gospel and three letters of John the apostle, pointing out several major stylistic differences. He writes, "From the ideas, and from the words and their arrangement, it may be reasonably conjectured that this one is different from that one." He notes, for example, that, whereas John the apostle never refers to himself by name in his gospel or letters, the John of Revelation frequently names himself as the author and seer (Revelation 1:1, 2, 4, 9; 22:7, 8). If he were the beloved disciple of Jesus, the brother of James, the one who had leaned on Jesus at the last supper, surely he would have made that explicit. He concludes that Revelation is not only "different from these writings but foreign to them; not touching, nor in the least bordering upon them; almost, so to speak, without even a syllable in common with them."[16]

Most scholars today would agree with Dionysius and Eusebius that the John of Revelation was not John the disciple of Jesus or the author of the Gospel of John. Beyond that, little is certain about this John of Patmos, as scholars have come to call him. The words of his text are his only remains, and so we are left to sift them for possible clues.

Lost in the Mail

Calling him John of Patmos is a little misleading, since he makes clear that he is writing while on that small island but is not from there. Rather he was there "because of the word of God and the testimony of Jesus," whatever that exactly means. Most assume he escaped there or was exiled there, perhaps from a city on the nearby mainland of Asia Minor, since all seven churches to which his seven letters are addressed reside there.

It is anachronistic to call the diverse early Jesus movement of the late first century CE "Christianity." As Pamela Eisenbaum makes clear in her *Paul Was Not a Christian*, "The vast majority of the twenty-seven documents that currently comprise the New Testament were written by Jews at a time before there was any such thing as Christianity. . . . As far as can be determined by historians, archeologists, and biblical scholars, there were no distinctively Christian institutions, buildings, or symbols in the first century."[17] These writings, moreover, including John's Revelation, often disagreed with one another about what it meant to be a Jewish follower of Jesus in the context of first-century Rome.

John's seven letters offer windows into where he stood amid this diversity of positions. Like Peter and James, who were leaders of the Jesus movement centered in Jerusalem, the letters suggest that John's was a practice-oriented religious perspective, concerned with purity through observance of Jewish law (or, at the very least, avoidance of specifically Gentile practices).[18] As James put it in his letter, "Just as the body without the spirit [or "breath"] is dead, so faith without works is also dead" (James 2:26). John would certainly have agreed. "I know your works," five of the seven letters begin (Revelation 2:2, 19; 3:1, 8, 15), and, throughout each, the focus is on faith in action. Specifically, he calls for Jewish observance and purity, harshly criticizing those who would "eat food sacrificed to idols" and those who have "soiled their clothes" (3:4) by sexual fornication (2:14, 20; 3:18), calling down judgment upon those followers of Jesus who "say they are Jews and are not," but rather are of the "synagogue of Satan" (2:9, 3:9; these may have been Gentile believers who claimed Jewish identity).

Now, contrast John's version of what we now call Christianity, with its emphasis on Jewish purity and resistance to assimilation, against the more accommodating version of the faith preached by Paul, "the apostle to the Gentiles," a few decades earlier. As other scholars have pointed out, Paul would likely have been on John's blacklist of false prophets and evildoers. "As to the eating of food offered to idols," for example, Paul tells the faithful in Corinth that, since "we know that no idol in the world really exists, and that 'there is no God but one,'" and since "food will not bring us close to God," therefore "we are no worse off if we do not eat, and no better off if we do" (1 Corinthians 8:4, 8). Yet, he adds, they should be careful with "this liberty" to eat food sacrificed to idols so as not to become a "stumbling block" to their weaker sisters and brothers.

Likewise, in his letter to the Galatians, Paul attacks rival teachers, "Judaizers" and "the circumcision faction," who were demanding converts to "live like Jews," which included being circumcised and not eating with Gentiles (Galatians 2:11–14). Speaking against James as well as John of Patmos, Paul declares that one is "justified by faith in Christ, and not by doing the works of the law, because no one will be justified by the works of the law" (2:16). As Elaine Pagels makes clear, "Those whom John says Jesus 'hates' look very much like Gentile followers of Jesus converted through Paul's teaching. . . . When we step back from John's angry rhetoric, we can see that the very practices John denounces are those that Paul had recommended."[19]

Monstrous Progeny

John's visions are very writerly. Not only are they driven by the oft-repeated divine command to write what he sees, but they are also composed around images of written texts in various forms: the seven letters to seven churches, the scroll with writing on front and back and sealed with seven seals, another scroll that John swallows, the "book of life" on which the names of the saints are written, and, of course, the "words of the prophecy of this book" (22:7, 10; cf. 22:9), which John insists must be kept and *not* sealed up, warning that anyone who adds or takes away anything from its words will suffer all the curses described therein.

Yet, as we noted earlier, much of what John "saw" and "wrote" he also must have heard and read before. For although Revelation is certainly unique among the writings of the New Testament, it is largely made from scriptural precursors. Well over half of Revelation's 404 verses include quotations, references, or allusions to other Jewish scriptures, the vast majority being from the prophets Ezekiel, Daniel, and Isaiah.[20] In other cases, John composes taunts and dirges over the anticipated fall of Rome, the new Babylon, as complex mash-ups of various prophetic lines and phrases about the demise of other ancient enemies. And in still other cases, he virtually copies and pastes whole chunks of others' prophetic visions into his own, as in his terrifying vision of the risen Christ, largely taken from Daniel. John writes,

> I saw one like the Son of Man, clothed [Greek *endedumenon*] with a long robe and with a golden sash across [or "around," *periezosmenon*] his chest. His head and his hair were white as white wool, white as snow; his eyes were like a flame of fire [*puros*], his feet were like burnished bronze, refined as in a furnace, and his voice was like the sound of many waters. In his right hand he held seven stars, and from his mouth came a sharp, two-edged sword, and his face was like the sun shining with full force. When I saw him, I fell at his feet as though dead. But he placed his right hand on me. (Revelation 1:13–17)

Now here is the Greek Septuagint version of Daniel's vision:

> I looked up and saw a man clothed [*endedumenos*] in linen, with a belt of gold from Uphaz around [*periezosmenos*] his waist. His body was like beryl, his face like lightning, his eyes like flaming torches [*puros*], his arms and legs like the gleam of burnished bronze, and the sound of his words like the roar of a multitude . . . and when I heard the sound of his

words, I fell into a trance, face to the ground. But then a hand touched me and roused me to my hands and knees. (Daniel 10:5–6, 9–10)

John, then, is no author in the way we moderns think about authorship, shaped as we are by half a millennium of print book culture. The media environment of print books and authors with which most of us are familiar differs radically from the media environment of early Christianity, in which handwritten scrolls and small codices of papyrus or animal skin were copied and shared within informal networks of communities who read them aloud when they met in houses for worship or study.

Within the canon of Christian scriptures, we are accustomed to thinking of John's collection of visions as a "book," like other books we know, a literary work of copyrightable intellectual property originating from and owned by a single author. But it is not. John's Revelation, or rather his revelations, are what Julia Kristeva would call an *intertextuality*, that is, an "intersection of textual surfaces," a field of quotations, paraphrases, and borrowed images from other texts and dialogues, all more or less consciously deployed, rearranged, revised, remixed, and so on.[21]

Likewise the writer himself: he is not some single, integrated whole, the author and origin of his work, but rather a dialogical space, a locus of intersecting voices and texts. And each of those intersecting voices and texts is likewise an intertextuality of other texts and voices, and so on, without end or beginning.

The literary text of Revelation is an intertextuality, an amalgamation of hundreds and hundreds of bits, pieces, and larger chunks from Jewish scriptures and other ancient Near Eastern and Greco-Roman mythologies, all stitched together, brought to life, and adopted by an otherwise unknown, unhomed visionary.

Revelation's birth, then, was not a "normal" one, at least not by modern standards. It was, as I suggested earlier, monstrous, like Dr. Frankenstein's creation: an amalgam of bits and pieces from other scriptural lives, dug up and sewn together to take on a life of its own. Its maker was less a parent than a reanimator, bidding his monstrous progeny to go forth and prosper. Thus, it is its biography, not John's, that we are pursuing.

Apocalypse Not Now

Augustine's Tale of Two Cities

If there is one thing that John of Patmos could not possibly have imagined, it is that Rome, the pinnacle of monstrously diabolical imperial might and the ultimate enemy of Christ and his true followers, would one day become so closely wedded to Christianity as to be synonymous with it—but that is what happened.

Indeed, no one could have imagined such a radical transformation of both Rome and Christianity even just a few years before it happened. In 303 CE, Emperor Diocletian published a royal edict calling for churches to be razed, their scriptures burned, and believers of high social rank demoted. That edict was soon followed by other decrees calling for the imprisonment of all Christian church leaders and forcing professed Christians to sacrifice to idols. Many dissenting Christians were tortured, oftentimes to death. Eusebius, who personally witnessed some of these atrocities, describes one man who, refusing to sacrifice to idols, was stripped naked, hoisted high, and beaten with rods until his bones shown through his skin. His torturers then put salt and vinegar on his wounds, after which "the remnants of his body, like flesh intended for eating, were placed on the fire, not at once, lest he should expire instantly, but a little at a time."[1]

To many Christians living through that period of severe persecution under Diocletian, it looked as though Revelation was finally coming horrifically true. As Eusebius put it, "He who had received power was seemingly aroused now as from a deep sleep," apparently alluding to Revelation's diabolical, blasphemous beast, who receives his kingdom and authority from the dragon "who is called the Devil and Satan" to kill any who refuse to worship his image (Revelation 12–16).[2] No doubt many believers found inspiration to resist Diocletian's edicts in Revelation's warnings that anyone who does not refuse such worship, even when faced with torture and death, will face far worse punishment from God.

Oxymoronic No More

Rome's campaign against Christianity lasted nearly a decade. And then, almost as suddenly as it had begun, it was over. In 313 CE, a year after the Western Roman Emperor Constantine purportedly dreamed of a fiery cross inscribed with the words "by this sign you shall conquer," he and the Eastern Roman Emperor Licinius signed the Edict of Milan, which mandated tolerance of Christianity, declaring that people were free to worship any deity as they saw fit.

Then, in 324 CE, after unifying the East and West under his rule, Constantine moved his capital to the predominantly Christian city of Byzantium, renaming it Constantinople. A year later, he further promoted and unified the Christian faith by convening the Council of Nicaea, which brought together bishops from throughout the empire in order to establish a strong consensus on doctrinal issues as well as matters of organizational structure and church hierarchy. And so the once precariously fringy and vulnerable early Jesus movement had become the Christendom of imperial state power. "Roman Christianity" was no longer an oxymoron.

The century following the establishment of Roman Christianity also saw the rapid establishment of a canon of Christian Scriptures, that is, an official, authoritative list of which texts were in and which were out for all Roman Christians. Canonization often coincides with other forms of institutionalization, and Christendom's increasingly hierarchical structures not only enabled but encouraged greater regulation and uniformity with regard to defining what counted as Scripture and what could be done with and said about it.

But there was another factor that led to the closing, more or less, of the Christian canon at this time: the development of the media technology of the big codex, or bound book, capable of holding all the texts in that canon together as a single volume. Although most scholars believe that Christianity was an early adopter of this new media technology, early codices were relatively small, not more than two hundred pages, with most being considerably smaller than that. By the late fourth century, however, the technology of the codex had advanced to the point of being able to hold an entire canon of Christian Scriptures. The most well-known example is the late fourth-century Codex Sinaiticus, which contained the entire Christian canon of the Old and New Testaments in Greek. Suffice it to say that the closing of the canon, the ability to collect and bind all of it into a single book, and the institutionalization of Roman Christendom are not mere coincidences; they went hand in hand. Empire plus codex equals canon.

How did Revelation relate to this new situation for the church? Given its fierce hatred for that very empire and desire for its downfall, how did this text, now increasingly embraced as an authored book, make it into the canon of Roman Christianity? Instead of going down in flames, its "whore of Babylon" was now wed to the church.

At the same time, Revelation's sense of urgency, assuring believers that it would all be over very soon, "for the time is near," did not carry as much freight as it had a couple of centuries before, especially as the church was now enjoying the comforts of state wealth and power. What then to do with Revelation?

One response, of course, was to leave this text and its violently anti-Roman fantasies behind. As we have already seen, its scriptural status had been a matter of debate from the beginning. While some, like Irenaeus, embraced it, others, like those mentioned by Dionysius of Alexandria, said it was senseless and veiled in ignorance. The fact that Eusebius includes it among the "disputed" texts that some accept and others reject in

325 CE makes clear that its questionable status had not been resolved by the time of Constantine's christening of the empire. With Rome now emerging as the imperial champion of Christendom rather than its monstrous enemy, there were good reasons to banish Revelation once and for all.

Another response to Revelation's identity crisis was to identify the text's enemy, Babylon, with something other than Rome: perhaps the diabolical forces of anti-God in Revelation are not those of the Roman empire per se; perhaps, instead, they are *doctrinal* enemies, heretics within the church.

In fact, as Elaine Pagels points out, the first bishop we know of to insist on including Revelation in the Christian canon, Athanasius of Alexandria, was especially good at othering his enemies with rhetoric adapted from that text.[3] Having ascended to his position as bishop with the blessing of Emperor Constantine but against the will of other leaders in Egypt, he faced decades of division and dissent. Indeed, much of his career was spent in exile, having been deposed by his rivals and attacking their positions only through missives.

Here is where Revelation came in handy as a means of establishing catholic (as in "universal") unity within the church against a common enemy—not Rome but doctrinal heretics. "In order to blaspheme our Lord Jesus Christ," Athanasius declared, his opponents were "mingling together their respective crimes, like the cup of Babylon," referring to "the cup full of abominations and the impurities" from which the whore of Babylon drinks while riding "a scarlet beast full of blasphemous names" in Revelation 17–18.[4]

In his famous Easter letter of 367 CE, Athanasius asserts as the only "genuine" and authoritative texts—for the first time, as far as we know—an official list of twenty-seven Christian writings that soon became the canon of the New Testament. Not surprisingly, given his embattled approach to such matters, he excludes all the other texts then circulating among Christians as heretical. Revelation caps off his list, which concludes with a warning that echoes the end of Revelation itself: "Let no man add to these, neither let him take ought from these."[5]

This approach, reading Revelation's diabolical Roman monsters as other kinds of enemies—theological, ideological, political, social, you name it—has continued to this day, as we will see. Revelation has proven to be a veritable *othering machine*: put my enemy in and he comes out infinitely more bad, an incarnation of ultimate evil, at which point it becomes clear that this cosmos is not big enough for the two of us.

But there was another challenge to Revelation's fitness for the new imperial Roman church: its questionable shelf life. "Blessed is the one who reads aloud the words of the prophecy, and blessed are those who hear and who keep what is written in it; for the time is near" (Revelation 1:3). "See, I am coming soon!" (20:7). "See, I am coming soon; my reward is with me, to repay according to everyone's work" (20:12). "'Surely I am coming soon.' Amen. Come, Lord Jesus!" (22:20). How long can you keep saying that the end is near, that Jesus will return to establish his kingdom any minute? And now, as Christ's former archenemy, according to Revelation, establishes its kingdom alongside the church, the signs of the times have changed quite dramatically.

What if the church were in it for the long haul? How to read Revelation in that light? How to extend its shelf life into a potentially much longer foreseeable future? It is here, at this very precarious moment in the life of Revelation, that Saint Augustine comes into the picture, offering a very different understanding of its timeline, one that gives it a much longer potential future.

Augustine's Early Years

Augustine of Hippo was born in 354 CE in the Roman municipality of Thagaste in northern Africa (modern-day Algeria). His mother, Monica, also a saint, was a devout Christian, and his father, Patricius, was a pagan with a hot temper who converted to Christianity on his deathbed, when Augustine was seventeen.

Augustine was very bright by all accounts and devoted himself to studies and teaching in rhetoric. Although raised by his mother to be a Christian, he explored other religious ideas and practices as a young man, including astrology and Manichaeism, a new religious movement of the time named for the Persian prophet Mani, who preached an elaborate dualism involving a cosmic struggle between the spiritual forces of light and the material forces of darkness and evil. Augustine was an avid evangelist for this movement throughout his twenties. When he moved to Milan, Italy, to teach at age twenty-nine, he was still under the sponsorship of the Manichaeans. There, however, he eventually became a disciple of the great Christian theologian Ambrose and, at age thirty-three, converted to Christianity.

Augustine also enjoyed an active love life early on, including several sexual affairs and a long-term committed relationship with a woman from Carthage with whom he had a son named Adeodatus. That union, however, was broken up by his mother when it became a hindrance to him marrying someone of his status. "My heart which clave unto her," he recalls in his *Confessions*, "was torn and wounded and bleeding." She left Adeodatus with him and his mother, vowing to God never to know another man. He, on the other hand, "not being so much a lover of marriage as a slave to lust," found another mistress while waiting for his betrothed, a ten-year-old girl, to reach the marriageable age of twelve.[6] Then, before that day came, in 387 CE, he and fourteen-year-old Adeodatus were baptized as Christians and became celibate. At once, Augustine recalls,

> anxiety for our past life vanished from us. . . . How did I weep, in Thy Hymns and Canticles, touched to the quick by the voices of Thy sweet-attuned Church! The voices flowed into mine ears, and the Truth distilled into my heart, whence the affections of my devotion overflowed, and tears ran down, and happy was I therein.[7]

Great Expectations

The priesthood of Augustine's time was essentially a popularity contest—though not the kind one necessarily wanted to win. Already attracting attention as an erudite preacher and teacher, Augustine became a priest by popular demand in 391 CE, and then a bishop in 395 CE of the relatively small, coastal city of Hippo, near his birthplace. The position of bishop was permanent, so he served in it until his death in 430 CE at age seventy-five.

It is difficult to imagine what Christianity would have looked like without Augustine, even if many would like to try. Doctrines such as original sin, creation *ex nihilo*, salvation by grace alone, and predestination, not to mention the church's deep distrust of human sexuality, all owe their early formulations to him. Having written more than five million words (that is how many have come down to us), his theological corpus is arguably more central to Christian doctrine than any other nonbiblical writings.

They are more central to doctrine than most biblical ones, too. Augustine had memorized the North African Latin text of the Old and New Testaments. As Garry Wills aptly puts it, "Augustine, like Ezekiel, or like the John of Revelation, had 'eaten' and afterward thought in its [Scripture's] terms and rhythms, with and through its words."[8] A master rhetorician, he had internalized not only the words and images of Christian Scriptures but their rhythms and cadences. His movements of thought and expression went with the flow of a biblical pool of imagination. In the process, his own writings effectively became scriptural, absorbing the Bible into theological ideas that the biblical texts themselves could never have conceived.

Augustine's home region of Northern Africa was what Paula Fredriksen calls the "Bible Belt" of the empire. Christians there were "at once severe and enthusiastic, fundamentalist and traditional in their biblical orientation."[9] They were proud of their resistance to the religious crackdowns of Diocletian, even in the face of severe persecutions. They revered their martyrs, compiled stories of their great acts, and held feast days to celebrate them.

Northern Africa was also a hotbed of millenarianism, believing that Christ would return very soon to defeat the enemies of God, raise the martyred saints from the dead, and establish his millennium-long reign on earth. Many believed that this reign would begin at the dawning of the seventh, or sabbatical, millennium of history since creation, and that the first six thousand years would soon be completed.

Exacerbating these millenarian expectations during Augustine's tenure as bishop was the rapid decline of the Roman Empire, which would ultimately fall in 476 CE when Flavius Odoacer deposed Emperor Romulus Augustus and became the first king of Italy. A decisive turn toward that ultimate end came in 410 CE when Rome was sacked by the Visigoths under King Alaric after he had taken many other cities in Greece and Italy.

The millenarian zeal of Augustine's time was anchored in a particular reading of one of John's visions toward the very end of Revelation, right before his culminating description of the new heaven, new earth, and new Jerusalem. Here is the scene:

> Then I saw an angel coming down from heaven, holding in his hand the key to the bottomless pit and a great chain. He seized the dragon, that ancient serpent, who is the Devil and Satan, and bound him for a thousand years, and threw him into the pit, and locked and sealed it over him, so that he would deceive the nations no more, until the thousand years were ended. After that he must be let out for a little while. Then I saw thrones, and those seated on them were given authority to judge. I also saw the souls of those who had been beheaded for their testimony to Jesus and for the word of God. They had not worshiped the beast or its image and had not received its mark on their foreheads or their hands. They came to life and reigned with Christ a thousand years. (The rest of the dead did not come to life until the thousand years were ended.) This is the first resurrection. Blessed and holy are those who share in the first resurrection. Over these the second death has no power, but they will be priests of God and of Christ, and they will reign with him a thousand years. (Revelation 20:1–6)

Augustine's millenarian opponents believed that this passage predicted the triumphal Second Coming of Christ. He would bind Satan, personified here as elsewhere in Revelation as a dragon, "that ancient serpent," and throw it into the bottomless pit (Greek *abussos*, "abyss") for a thousand years. Those Christian ancestors who had been martyred for their faith would then be brought back to life in a "first resurrection" and would reign alongside Christ.

Then, at the end of that thousand-year reign, these Christian millenarians believed that Satan would be let loose for three and a half years, and would gather the nations from the four corners of the earth for battle against Christ and his saints (20:7–8). In that battle, Satan's armies would be defeated once and for all, and he would be thrown into the lake of fire to be tortured forever.

Finally, according to this millenarian reading of Revelation, there would be a second resurrection and Last Judgment, in which all the dead would be brought back to life and "judged according to their works" (20:12). Those found unrighteous would be condemned to a "second death" of eternal damnation, whereas the righteous would dwell forever with God in the new heaven and new earth, with its gleaming capital, the new Jerusalem, as described in John's culminating vision (ch. 21–22).

Within this millenarian scenario, the Second Coming of Christ, the binding of Satan, the resurrection of the martyrs, and the thousand-year reign were just around the corner. Apocalypse now. What came instead was Augustine's theological masterwork, *The City of God*. Written over the course of more than a decade, from 413 to 426 CE, this text reads the book of Revelation into a radically different historical scenario, one that puts off the return of Christ for centuries, at least. With it, Augustine effectively hit the long-term snooze button on apocalyptic expectations. Apocalypse not now. Not yet. Not for a long time.[10]

Two Cities

Commonly known as *The City of God* (full title *De Civitate Dei contra Paganos* [The city of God against pagans]), it is really a tale of two cities, representing two communities of humankind. On the one hand, there is the city of this world—earthly, bound to time, ever-changing, perishable, predestined for eternal damnation. On the other hand, there is the city of God—heavenly, eternal, changeless, imperishable, "predestined to reign eternally with God."[11] While all are born into the city of the world, Augustine explains, the elect are predestined to be born again into the city of God through baptism in Christ.

In the present age, the tales of these two cities are intertwined, their populations intermixed. For now, it is impossible to separate the elect of the city of God from the damned of the city of the world. So it is even in the Christian church, for "in this wicked world . . . there are many reprobate mingled with the good, and both are gathered together by the gospel as in a drag net" (18.49).

Here is where Revelation begins to show itself as key to Augustine's schema: the two cities will not be sorted out until the "second resurrection" and Last Judgment described therein, when all the dead will be resurrected and judged. On the one hand, the elect, true citizens of the city of God, will reign with God forever; on the other hand, the damned, also true citizens of the city of the world, will undergo the "second death" of eternal punishment in hell with the Devil. For, Augustine writes, "they who do not belong to this city of God shall inherit

eternal misery, which is also called the second death, because the soul shall then be separated from God its life,
and therefore cannot be said to live, and the body shall be
subjected to eternal pains" (19.28).

What then of the "first resurrection" of the saints, also
described in Revelation, the one inaugurated by the glorious coming of Christ with whom they will reign for a
thousand years? This, Augustine says, has *already happened* in the death and resurrection of Jesus Christ and
the establishment of his church. For the "first resurrection" of the saints is not to be understood as a resurrection of the body but of the soul, that is, the saving grace of
Christ through his atoning sacrifice on the cross. This is
why it is written that "over these the second death has no
power, but they will be priests of God and of Christ, and
they will reign with him a thousand years" (Revelation
20:6). They have been saved from death to eternal salvation. Thus, Augustine summarizes:

> As, then, there are two regenerations, of which I have
> already made mention—the one according to faith,
> and which takes place in the present life by means of
> baptism; the other according to the flesh, and which
> shall be accomplished in its incorruption and immor-
> tality by means of the great and final judgment—so
> are there also two resurrections—the one the first and
> spiritual resurrection, which has place in this life, and
> preserves us from coming into the second death; the
> other the second, which does not occur now, but in
> the end of the world, and which is of the body, not of

the soul, and which by the last judgment shall dismiss some into the second death, others into that life which has no death. (19.6)

But what about "that ancient serpent," Satan, whom Christ shuts in the abyss "so that he would deceive the nations no more, until the thousand years were ended" (Revelation 20:3)? This abyss, Augustine explains, is not literal but figurative, a "place away from God and the saints in this world. . . . By the abyss is meant the countless multitude of the wicked whose hearts are unfathomably deep in malignity against the Church of God" (19.7). The abyss, then, is simply in the company of abysmal people, whom Satan now possesses more fully than ever, since he may no longer deceive the souls of God's elect, whom Augustine identifies as "the nations" Satan can no longer deceive.

So Satan has been bound, insofar as he cannot touch the ultimate salvation of the citizens of the city of God. Yet he still brings suffering and temptation to this world, intermixed as it is with good and evil, light and darkness. Likewise, divine judgment is already happening, even though it may be difficult to perceive in a world where good and bad are so entangled with one another. Such is our uncertain time of intermingling, in which, it seems, the righteous suffer and the wicked prosper. But all this ambiguity and intermixing will ultimately be cleared up at the Last Judgment, "because in it there shall be no room left for the ignorant questioning why this wicked person is happy and that righteous man unhappy" (20.1).

So, for Augustine, the glorious coming of Christ described in Revelation 20 has already happened. Christ *now* reigns with the church. That millennium is not soon to begin, as millenarians believed; it is already well underway. But how long will this millennial reign of Christ with the church last? Will it be literally one thousand years, after which time the world will enter into its seventh, sabbatical millennium without end? Perhaps. Or perhaps it is a figurative term, "the number of perfection to mark the fullness of time," thus referring to the total duration of this world from beginning to end (21.7). In any case, Augustine insists, it is vanity to presume that anyone can determine the precise number of years, since Jesus himself said to his disciples that "about that day or hour no one knows, neither the angels in heaven, nor the Son, but only the Father" (Mark 13:32). Nor can anyone sort out the citizens of God's holy city from the damned rest of humankind, even in the church itself, until that time.

New Heaven, New Earth, New Bodies

The church will continue to reign, says Augustine, even during those penultimate three and a half years when Satan will "burst forth from lurking hatred into open persecution," gathering an army from the four corners of the earth to battle Christ's saints (Revelation 20:7–10). Not that God will seclude them entirely from persecution, but he will not permit Satan to touch their "inner man, where faith resides." Thus, by withstanding less perilous "outward temptation," they will grow stronger in their faith (20.8).

When the three and a half years are finished, Christ and his armies will defeat Satan and his armies once and for all. Then will come the "second resurrection," that is, of all the dead, who will be subjected to Christ's Last Judgment. The unrighteous whose names are not found in the book of life will be sent straight to hell—what Revelation calls "the lake of fire," where Satan and the beasts will already be (Revelation 20:10, 15).

The new heaven and new earth will not *replace* the former heaven and earth, but rather will be the *purification* of them—the city of God now disentangled once and for all from the city of worldly sin and evil. In the same moment, the righteous will be purged of their fallenness and mortality as well, thereby becoming worthy citizens of the heavenly city, "so that, as the world itself is renewed to some better thing, it is fitly accommodated to men, themselves renewed in their flesh to some better thing" (20.16).[12]

Complicating Matters

Anticipating questions from skeptical readers, Augustine is particularly concerned to address potential complications with regard to both the mass judgment and the mass resurrection he expects will take place.

The first issue concerns the media technology that will be employed: what kind codex will this "book of life" be? How massive would it have to be in order to hold all those names, and how tediously long and awkward would it be to look through it, one name at a time, for the record of every human being that has ever lived? "Shall there be present as many angels as men, and shall each man hear his life recited by the angel assigned to him?" No, he reasons, because the text indicates only one book and that scenario would require separate books for everyone. Rather, Augustine explains, it will be a book of "a certain divine power" such that when it is opened, every individual will immediately recall in a single flash of clarity all of her or his works, good and bad, and in the same moment will know what her or his judgment must be. "And this divine power is called a book, because in it we shall as it were read all that it causes us to remember" (20.14).[13]

Second, in what form will the dead be resurrected? Key here is Augustine's expectation that the resurrected body will be a *perfection* and *completion* of the formerly fallen body into an ideal one suited for the purified city of God. Thus, for example, those who died as infants will be resurrected to their fully matured, "perfect stature," which was theirs "potentially, though not in actual bulk," from birth. For "the child who is to be tall or short is already tall or short" in potential. Indeed, Augustine writes, even if that infant's potential is to be taller than Jesus Christ himself, he will be resurrected to that height (22.14–15). Likewise, those who died young will be raised to the age they would have reached in their prime. Those who died past their prime, on the other hand, will not be restored to that younger age, but the frailties of their old age will be removed.

What about the sexes of the resurrected? Presuming, as Augustine does, based on his reading of Genesis 2, that the first woman was created from the first man's rib and is therefore derivative, will women be raised as men? No, he explains, because it is not sexual difference but sexual desire that is the fallen state of humankind. Before the fall, they were "naked and not ashamed" (Genesis 2:25), that is, nonsexual but not nonsexed. "The sex of woman is not a vice," therefore, "but nature. . . . He who created both sexes will restore both" (22.17).

And what about hair and nails—the stuff on bodies that grows and gets trimmed off in the course of life? After all, Jesus said, "Not a hair of your head shall perish" (Luke 21:18). Does this mean that all the trimmed parts will be restored to resurrected people, like bizarre extensions on their fingers and heads? No, Augustine says. We should think of hair and nails in terms of number, not length. If a person lost hair or nails in life, the original number of hairs and nails will be restored, at normal length. Bald people will get all their hair back, but not all its length. Likewise people who were obese or emaciated in life will be restored to their ideal proportions and, we can presume, body mass index. Also, blemishes, scars, and other marks on the body will be removed, restoring each person to her or his ideal form—with the singular exception of the wounds of martyrs, which Augustine says are not deformities but marks of honor that "will add lustre to their appearance, and a spiritual, if not a bodily beauty" (22.19).

Finally, Augustine addresses the greatest challenge to his interpretation of the resurrection of the dead. That is, the fact that dead bodies decay, turn to dust, get eaten by animals, consumed by fire, or turned to liquid. How can a dead person's "dissolved elements" be regathered to reconstitute her or his body? Even more consternating, what about a person who has been eaten by another person? How can an eaten body be restored, "for it has been converted into the flesh of the man who used it as his nutriment" (22.12)?

Augustine's solution is something of a theological prototheory of the conservation of mass. Whatever was lost to decay or liquefaction will be restored to its original body. Even the flesh of the person that got eaten, he asserts, will be returned to its original body, "for it must be looked upon as borrowed by the other person, and, like a pecuniary loan, must be returned to the lender." But where will this payback leave the cannibal, now short on flesh? The flesh that he lost to hunger went into the air through evaporation. So God will recall it from the atmosphere and restore it to its original owner, as well (22.20).

From Genesis to Revelation

Augustine's extended deliberations on the logistics of mass resurrection and last judgment may seem unnecessary to his larger theological treatise on the city of God. But, in fact, they are essential, insofar as they are part of the work of integrating his reading of Revelation, where these complications arise, with his larger presentation of the whole history of creation, from Genesis to Revelation. The Nicene Creed, which was already the universal Christian profession of faith during his time, confessed belief in "the resurrection of the body" and the expectation that Christ would return "to judge the quick and the dead." In *The City of God*, the Second Coming, the "second resurrection," the Last Judgment, and the new heaven and new earth in the last chapters of Revelation become an explication of those professions.

And so, Augustine effectively integrated John's apocalypse, or rather pieces of it, into a grand biblical narrative of the history of creation as the ultimate conclusion to his tale of two cities. At the same time, he gave it a new, millennium-long shelf life, thereby securing its place as Scripture, at least for the foreseeable future.

Cry Out and Write

Hildegard's Apocalypse

Augustine gave Revelation a new, millennium-long lease on life as the interpretive key to his tale of two cities. The city of God would endure alongside the city of the world until the Last Judgment, at which time good and evil would be sorted out. Then the citizens of the fallen, unredeemed world would be cast into hell for eternal punishment, and the citizens of the city of God would assume their perfect heavenly bodies and reign with Christ forever over a new heaven and new earth. This would be the very culmination of history, predestined and willed by God since the beginning of creation.

Thus, in this understanding of John's vision, the Second Coming was not still coming but had already come with the resurrection of Christ and the beginning of his church. His millennial reign was well underway, and it would continue for a good long time.

Y1K

As was the case for the world approaching "Y2K," a popular acronym for "Year 2000," there was much apocalyptic fervor and speculation as the church approached and then passed the end of its first millennium, and it often involved images and ideas associated with Revelation.[1] Would the city of God's cohabitation with the city of the world last exactly one thousand years? If so, when exactly did it begin? Or does that number simply represent a really long time? In which case, how can we know when that period is over, at which time "that ancient serpent who is the Devil and Satan" will be released and begin his three-and-a-half-year persecution of the church? How, moreover, will he appear? As an actual dragon? Or is that, too, a figure of something less literally serpentine and diabolical? Perhaps he will come disguised as a charming king, or charismatic priest. Perhaps even as the Pope himself.

The European late Middle Ages before and after the turn of the millennium were rife with political and ecclesiastical conflict, corruption, and schism. If a king did not like the Pope, he might appoint his own "antipope."[2] It was also a time of fervent religious reform and apocalyptic expectation, calling for theological invention and innovation. The rotting fruit on the vines of church and empire invited visions of a great reaping, purifying and perfecting the city of God in preparation for the dawn of a new divine era.

Central here was a particular concept of Christian prophecy. Harking back to the Hebrew biblical prophets, especially as they were grafted into the apocalyptic imaginary of Revelation, medieval religious visionaries, orthodox and heterodox alike, saw a divine plan at work in the mess of history, and they believed that particular people and historical events of their day were encoded signs from God that could be decoded with the help of Scripture.[3]

Within this context of fervent apocalyptic vision, scenes from Revelation continued to serve as core visual vocabulary for such prophesying. It linked into a number of extremely popular apocalyptic writings that provided lenses for interpreting religious leaders as monstrous enemies of God and events as signs of Christ's immanent return. Particularly influential in conjunction with Revelation's images of the Last Judgment were early Christian prophetic texts now known as the Sibylline Oracles. These texts, believed to be oracles delivered by ancient sibyls, women with divinely inspired visionary powers, date back as early as the fourth century and were extremely popular throughout the Middle Ages, simultaneously building upon and built from the apocalyptic visions of Revelation.[4]

In the seventh-century Syrian *Apocalypse of Pseudo-Methodius*, for example, a long-dead emperor returns to defeat the Ishmaelites (Muslims) and establish Christian rule. After an extended period of thriving in the land, Gog and Magog, enemies of Christ's armies in Revelation (20:7–10; also named as enemies of God in Ezekiel), rise up against the righteous, causing massive bloodshed and destruction before the captain of Christ's angels defeats them. The emperor expects that this defeat will lead to the arrival of the Antichrist, so he goes to Jerusalem to await him. When the Antichrist appears, the emperor places his crown on top of the cross on which Christ was crucified, and the crowned cross soars up into the heavens. The emperor dies, and the Antichrist begins his terrible reign until, suddenly, the cross reappears in the sky, signaling the glorious return of Christ, the ultimate defeat of the Antichrist, and the Last Judgment.[5] Here, as throughout the traditions of the Sibylline Oracles, we see roots and stems of Revelation grafted into new visions that extend the reach of apocalyptic spirituality in the late Middle Ages.

In this chapter and the next, we focus on two roughly contemporary apocalyptic visionaries who brought new life to Revelation within this context of the dawn of the second millennium: Hildegard of Bingen (1098–1179) and Joachim of Fiore (c. 1135–1202). Although contemporaries, they did not know one another. Indeed, there is no evidence that either ever even heard of the other, yet they had a great deal in common. Both were Benedictine monastics (part of communities following the sixth-century Rule of Saint Benedict), and both advocated for dramatic reforms in that tradition as well as in the Catholic church broadly. Both were early espousers of spiritual *meliorism*, which, against Augustine, insisted that this world, though corrupt, could and should improve itself in anticipation of the coming Last Judgment.[6] Both developed elaborately complex apocalyptic thought worlds based on Revelation and other prophetic texts. Finally, and perhaps most significantly for this biography of Revelation, both were highly visual "picture thinkers," whose image-rich descriptions of their visions were accompanied by lavish illustrations that were in many respects more popular and influential than their written texts—even to this day.

> And behold! In the forty-third year of my earthly
> course, as I was gazing with great fear and trembling
> attention at a heavenly vision, I saw a great splendor
> in which resounded a voice from Heaven, saying,
> "Oh fragile woman, ashes of ashes, and filth of filth!
> Say and write what you see and hear!"[7]

So begins Hildegard of Bingen's preface to her first and most influential work, the *Scivias* (short for *Scito vias Domini* [Know the ways of the Lord]), a series of twenty-six apocalyptic visions, ten years in the making, that take us from the beginning of creation to the Last Judgment and the redemption of the world in richly descriptive language that itself cries out for illustration.

Indeed, it is likely that her *Scivias* was from the beginning a multimedia project, integrating word and image on its pages. The oldest known manuscript, which was done in the scriptorium of Hildegard's convent around 1165, already included the thirty-five miniature illustrations that most editions of the work include to this day.[8] It is even possible that she sketched her visions while dictating them to her beloved tutor and secretary Volmar. The illustration in the prologue, in which she receives her call to prophesy, depicts her holding a wax pad and stylus, her head enveloped in red tongues of flame while Volmar looks on attentively with a codex in his hand. The way she holds the stylus, almost like a brush, suggests she may not be writing but sketching, describing to

FIGURE 4.1. Hildegard enveloped in the fire of the Holy Spirit while describing (and perhaps drawing) her vision to her companion Volmar, an illumination accompanying the Prologue of her *Scivias*; facsimile of miniature from the Rupertsberg Codex, late twelfth century.

Volmar in spoken word what she is depicting with stylus on the pad.

While her revelations are highly imagistic, calling them "visions" does not adequately represent the way she describes her own experience of them. What she "sees" and "hears," she explains, are not words or images per se, but rather a "fiery light of exceeding brilliance" that "permeated my whole brain, and inflamed my whole heart and my whole breast."[9] Such personal accounts of her rapturous experiences have convinced some, including the late neurologist Oliver Sacks, that her visions must have derived from the auras and visual scotomata of migraine headaches. But Sacks, a deeply thoughtful student of the "paradox of disease," well understood how such physiological experiences, however "banal, hateful or meaningless to the majority of people, can become, in a privileged consciousness, the substrate of a supreme ecstatic inspiration."[10] So it was, he believed, with Hildegard.

In such experiences, Hildegard recalls, she suddenly discerned, or "tasted" (*sapiebam*), the full explication of all Scripture—not in deciphering and dividing its syllables and words but in sensing its meaning in her whole self. What Hildegard unfolds and refracts into highly elaborate explications of biblical history, then, is an embodied, aesthetic experience that involves not only seeing and hearing but also smelling, touching, and tasting in a way that for her comprehends all of sacred time and space, from the moment of creation to its final culmination. She was an aesthetic theologian, proceeding sensually toward a total theology of creation—past, present, and future.

Although Hildegard had had these ecstatic experiences since childhood, she did not begin work on her *Scivias* until the age of forty-three, in 1141, five years after the death of her abbess Jutta von Sponheim. Jutta, who was six years older than Hildegard, had been her mentor and teacher. Hildegard had come under her care as an oblate at the age of fourteen. A fervent ascetic, Jutta taught Hildegard to read and write, and she was central to her spiritual formation. Perhaps being released from Jutta's discipleship and replacing her as *magistra*, or master teacher, in their community of nuns empowered Hildegard to share her own revelations.

In fact, you could say that the death of Jutta marked the beginning of a second, astonishingly productive career for Hildegard. Not only did she subsequently found two convents, one at a river crag called Rupertsberg in Bingen am Rhine, Germany, in 1150, and one in Eibingen, Germany, in 1165, but she also published a veritable library of writings. In addition to her *Scivias*, which she finished at age fifty-three, she wrote a major book of ethics (*Liber vitae meritorium* [The book of life's merits]), another book on cosmology (*Liber divinorum operum* [The book of divine works]), two lives of saints, the first known morality play (*Ordo Virtutum* [Order of the virtues]), seventy musical compositions for liturgy, numerous sermons and essays, several hundred letters, and an encyclopedia of science and naturopathic medicine. All the while, she gained greater and greater popularity as a theological and medical advisor as well as a political and ecclesiastical critic. She was the Martin Luther of the late

Middle Ages; or rather Luther was the Hildegard of the Reformation.

She did all this, moreover, in a religious culture that placed huge constraints on women. They were prohibited from priestly roles and increasingly discouraged from preaching and religious counseling. They were also excluded from the scholastic systems that were emerging at the time. Beneath all these constraints was a widespread fascination with and fear of what were believed to be the dangerous powers of women's bodies—a belief that Hildegard herself seemed at times to share, celebrating the power of virginity as a form of independence from patriarchy and the denigration of female sexuality. As medieval cultural historian Carolyn Walker Bynum puts it, her *Scivias* "scintillates with a concern for embodiment—as both glorious and deplorable."[11]

Write What You See

The book of Revelation and other biblical writings, including the creation stories of Genesis, the prophets, and the Psalms, comprised the deepest parts of Hildegard's pool of apocalyptic imagination. Yet she did not know them primarily as books, or parts of a book called the Bible, but as elements in the Benedictine ritual practice of scriptural reading, meditation, prayer, and contemplation called *lectio divina*, through which she memorized, or better internalized, many small snippets of Scripture in the standard Latin translation known as the Vulgate, along with other religious writings. Over time, this ever-growing and deepening field of intertextual resonances became part of her very being. Anne Clark aptly describes Hildegard's process as "ruminative interpretation, where she circles back to favorite themes and texts, unafraid of uncovering divergent meanings from the same passage, coupling seemingly unrelated texts."[12]

It was in this context that Revelation found new life. Indeed, Hildegard's embodied, ruminative imagination was an ideal host for its meme-like, story-shaped images, themselves largely drawn from earlier biblical texts, allowing them to circulate and attach to larger constellations that formed the visions described and depicted in her *Scivias*.

Hildegard's own highly self-conscious, writerly prophetic identity carries strong echoes of John of Patmos. Both John and Hildegard begin their call narratives with descriptions of an ecstatic experience followed by a voice commanding them to *write* what they *see*: whereas John writes that he "was in the spirit on the Lord's day, and I heard behind me a loud voice like a trumpet saying 'Write in a book what you see'" (Revelation 1:9–10), Hildegard writes that she was "gazing with great fear and trembling" at a "heavenly vision" when she "saw a great splendor in which resounded a voice from heaven, saying to me, 'Say and write what you see and hear.'"[13] For Hildegard, like John but unlike earlier Hebrew prophets, prophecy was not a live oracular performance but a textual production.

Hildegard also frames many of her visionary experiences with phrases unique to Revelation: three of her visions begin with the phrase, "After this I looked, and behold" (*Post haec vidi et ecce*), which is identical to the Latin Vulgate text of Revelation 4:1 and 15:15; and seven other of her visions begin with the shorter phrase "After this I looked" (*Post haec vidi*), which is identical to Revelation 7:1, 7:9, and 18:1.[14] She also uses most of John's unique terminology and imagery for Satan, whom she, like John, describes as a deceptive dragon and "ancient serpent" (*serpentem antiquum*).[15]

Beyond such echoes in style and vocabulary, Hildegard shares John's spatial-temporal imagination. Her visions, like those of Revelation, are elaborate scenes or series of interconnected scenes in which human and divine beings interact and transform across space and time. We find this mode of description and depiction throughout the three books of the *Scivias*, from the image of creation in Book 1 as a cosmic egg with many complex layers or folds, each structured as a balance of oppositions with every element carrying both natural and theological meaning, through the last visions of Book 3, which present the glorious culmination of history in the binding of Satan, the Last Judgment, and the new heaven and earth in the form of a vast structure called the Building of Salvation.

The Building of Salvation

Constructed as an eclectic amalgam of elements from Ezekiel's vision of the new Jerusalem and its temple as well as John's vision of the walled city of the new Jerusalem in

FIGURE 4.2. The Building of Salvation, an illumination accompanying Hildegard's *Scivias* 3.2; facsimile of miniature from the Rupertsberg Codex, late twelfth century.

Revelation (which is itself drawn from Ezekiel 40–47), Hildegard's edifice is simultaneously a four-walled city and a four-walled rectangular building, with bulwarks on the corners that face east, west, north, and south. Encircling this walled edifice is another wall, made partly of shining light and partly of stone, that reaches all the way from the heights down into the abyss. The building itself is founded upon a mountain attached to an immeasurably large stone over which God sits enthroned.

Every element of this building carries theological symbolism. Hildegard explains that the mountain, for example, represents the history of the faithful, beginning with Abraham's covenant with God and culminating with the incarnation of Christ. The stone to which the mountain is attached represents the fear of the Lord, on which faith itself depends. The encircling wall of shining light and stone stands for protection from temptation for the faithful within, with the light representing speculation and clear thinking about what is right and the stone representing good works. The four walls of the city draw the multitudes of faithful from the four corners of the earth to divine grace and also are the "four categories of faith," namely: Noah, who followed God simply by choosing good over evil; Abraham, who abided by the covenant of circumcision; Moses, the giver and follower of divine law; and the Son of God, from whom the "inner shoot" of the Church arose. Here we see a kind of protodispensationalism—the idea of human history moving through a series of different dispensations of divine grace—which her contemporary, Joachim of Fiore, will develop much further, as we will see.

The building's four corners, Hildegard continues, also represent essential theological elements in the salvation of humankind: the eastern corner is the incarnation of God in the Son so that justice could arise in humankind; the western corner is salvation by faith; the northern corner is the promise of grace for fallen humankind; and the southern corner is the restoration of humankind by which "the ardent work of God and man bore full fruit."

The painting that accompanies this description is a perspective-defying, top-down view of the encircled and walled city. Its towers and walls are all splayed out flat on the ground but still joined at the corners. The space inside the walls is empty, but on the walls themselves are various characters. Some, notably the Son of God who sits at the top of the image on the northern corner, have already been discussed in the text (although he was identified with the eastern corner, not the northern one). Others, notably the "jealousy" or "zeal of God," an angry-faced bald head with three giant wings hovering at the western corner, have yet to be described.

After describing and depicting the building as a whole, the next eight visions explicate, in words and images that sometimes conflict, its different elements: the Tower of Anticipation of God's Will (3.3), the Pillar of the Word of God (3.4), the Jealousy of God (3.5), the Stone Wall of the Old Law (3.6), the Pillar of the Trinity (3.7), the Pillar of the Savior's Humanity (3.8), the Tower of the Church (3.9), and finally the Son of Man and the Five Virtues (3.10).[16]

This, then, is no ordinary building but a storied architecture of Christian history and theology that provides not only a diachronic outline of the grand narrative of salvation but also a synchronic diagram of the virtues of the Church that are needed for salvation.

We Are Now in the Seventh Millennium

Once the building has been fully explicated in stunning literary and visual detail, Hildegard turns her attention to the final three visions of the *Scivias*, which depict and describe the demise of the Antichrist after a time of tribulation (3.11), the Last Judgment and the new heaven and earth (3.12), and, finally, the glorious scene of the Symphony of Praise (3.3).

At this point, Hildegard's sense of apocalyptic urgency around her own moment in history intensifies, as does her sense of prophetic calling. In keeping with earlier Christian apocalyptic expectations, including Augustine's interpretation of the millennial reign and Second Coming in Revelation, Hildegard parallels the seven days of creation in Genesis with the seven millennia of world history.[17] As Christ explains to her,

> In six days God completed His works, and on the seventh he rested. What does this mean? The six days are the six numbered epochs; and in the sixth epoch the latest miracles were brought forth in the world, as God finished His work on the sixth day. But now the world is in the seventh epoch, approaching the end of time, as on the seventh day. (3.11)

The world is now in its seventh, or sabbath, millennium, which corresponds to the seventh day of creation, when God had finished working and took the first Sabbath rest. In this stillness of divine activity, she laments, the Catholic church languishes.

> But now the Catholic faith wavers among the nations and the Gospel limps among the people . . . and the food of life, which is the divine Scriptures, cools to tepidity. For this reason, I now speak through a person who is not eloquent in the Scriptures or taught

by an earthly teacher; I Who Am speak through her
of new secrets and mystical truths, heretofore hidden
in books, like one who mixes clay and then shapes it
to any form he wishes. (3.11)

Weakened by trials and tribulations, and lacking suste-
nance from Scripture that has gone lukewarm ("*tepidus*,"
the very same word used to describe the church of Laodicea in Revelation 3:16), the church falters and loses its way.
Therefore God has called Hildegard to prophesy through
mysteries once hidden in books but now revealed in her
new literary-visual form of the *Scivias*.

At the center of Hildegard's vision of the Catholic
church's tribulation under the tyranny of the Antichrist
sits an overwhelmingly violent, misogynistic three-part
depiction and description of a woman being sexually as-
saulted by a monstrous head. Here she combines three
dimensions of the book of Revelation—misogyny, sexual
violation, and desecration—into an unprecedented and
shocking literary-visual image:

And from her waist to the place that denotes the female, she had various scaly blemishes; and in that latter place was a black and monstrous head. It had fiery
eyes, and ears like an ass', and nostrils and mouth like
a lion's; it opened wide its jowls and terrible clashed
its horrible iron-colored teeth. And from this head
down to her knees, the figure was white and red, as if
bruised by many beatings; and from her knees to her
tendons where they joined her heels, which appeared
white, she was covered with blood.

FIGURE 4.3. The Antichrist's persecution of the Church and ultimate downfall (bottom frame), an illumination accompanying
Scivias 3.11; facsimile of miniature from the Rupertsberg Codex,
late twelfth century.

This, Hildegard later explains, represents the Catholic
church's persecution during the seventh millennium by the
Antichrist, whom she identifies as the beast of Revelation.

This persecution will continue, she explains, until the
arrival of "the two witnesses of Truth," recalling the two

witnesses who are killed but then resurrected in Revelation (11:3–13). Explicating John's description of one of the beast's heads being mortally wounded but then healed, Hildegard writes that it is actually a sleight-of-hand, a magic trick to fake the power of resurrection: "By his lying arts he will pretend he is pouring out his blood in death . . . but he will not fall in the body but in a deceiving shadow" (3.11).

This filthy, ferocious figure will attempt to bring his assault to heaven itself, but will be destroyed once and for all, an act that will bring an end to his tyranny and inaugurate the Last Judgment. The violence against the woman who represents the Catholic church continues as the beast rips himself from her crotch, covered in feces:

> That monstrous head moved from its place with such a great shock that the figure of the woman was shaken through all her limbs. And a great mass of excrement adhered to the head; and it raised itself up upon a mountain and tried to ascend the height of Heaven. And behold, there came suddenly a thunderbolt, which struck the head with such great force that it fell from the mountain and yielded up its spirit in death. (3.11)

The illustration of this vision (the bottom frame in Figure 4.3) can scarcely capture the horror let alone the complexity of Hildegard's text. It depicts three separate acts within one frame, moving from the top left to the top right to the bottom right, something like the way a comic book might narrate consecutive scenes. First, on the upper left-hand side of the frame, the Antichrist qua horned, bloodshot-eyed, furry-faced beast grins toothily from between the legs of the church qua woman, her head crowned as royalty, her arms held open in a gesture of helplessness or worship. Second, in the upper right-hand corner, the same head perches atop a tall, narrow mountain, floating in a cloud of excrement. Finally, in the lower right-hand corner, it sinks sideways into the mire, still grinning eerily.

By setting illustration alongside text, Hildegard's *Scivias* invites conscious reflection on the very different rhetorical potentials of word and image. Here, as with John's vision of "the one like the Son of Man" before whom he falls on his face as if dead (1:12–16), description defies depiction. Like many of the visions in the book of Revelation, those Hildegard is describing are practically unimaginable. Her written words combine series of mutually incompatible elements (images, sounds) in ways that one simply cannot picture, in the mind or on paper, without leaving things out. Paradoxically, her literary visions are often revelations of things that defy visual revelation. The parts add up to more than any comprehensible whole.

Purifying the World

This sense of the incomprehensibility of Hildegard's revelations continues into the next vision, the Last Judgment and the new heaven and earth. It begins with the total consummation and purification of all of creation: "For the fire displaces all the air, and the water engulfs all the earth; and thus all things are purified, and whatever is foul in the world vanishes as if it had never been, as salt disappears when it is put into water" (3.12). Then, in this empty space of scorched earth, the dead are raised, emerging from the ground, coming back together into whole persons, and being rewrapped in flesh.

Christ then returns to judge them all in an image that combines John's vision of "one like the Son of Man" at the beginning of Revelation with Christ's enthronement for the Last Judgment at the end.

> And suddenly from the East a great brilliance shone forth; and there, in a cloud, I saw the Son of Man, with the same appearance He had had in the world and with His wounds still open, coming with the angelic choirs. He sat upon a throne of flame, glowing but not burning, which floated on the great tempest which was purifying the world. (3.12)

Christ blesses those marked as good and ushers them into heaven, and he sends the others to eternal damnation with the Devil and his angels in hell, "as it is written in the same place," namely the end of Revelation.

Thence forward, the earth will have been "transformed into great calm and beauty," its natural forces no longer harmful, its rough places made plain. And there, she concludes, again quoting "My beloved John" as witness, there will be no dark of night but only light of day (Revelation 22:5), because God's glory will illumine all.

So ends the world on its last day of its seventh millennium, and so begins the new era of eternal life in the brilliant presence of God. But this is not the end of Hildegard's *Scivias*. She concludes with one more vision (3.13), which incorporates not only word and image but also and especially music. Indeed, as Barbara J. Newman puts it, this last scene is not so much a vision as it is a concert.[18]

First, Hildegard offers fourteen songs in the form of an antiphon and a responsory to the Virgin Mary, to the nine orders of angelic beings, to the prophets, to the martyrs, to the confessors, and to the virgins. Then she offers a lament and a prayer of intercession on behalf of the unsaved; then a dramatic play that portrays the soul's pilgrimage from innocence through temptation to overcoming the Devil; then a brief reflection on the power of music; and finally an allegorical reading of Psalm 150 in which the musical instruments in the psalm symbolize different kinds of saints (prophets, apostles, martyrs, confessors, and virgins).

Here, too, in the musical compositions of her final coda to the *Scivias*, Hildegard resonates with the book of Revelation, where voices speak like trumpets and where the four living creatures, twenty-four elders with harps, and the myriads and myriads of angels are always breaking out in songs of praise. Both Revelation and the *Scivias* are forms of musical theater—liturgical apocalypses that proceed through ritual performance structured around song.

Living Beyond

The new life given to Revelation in Hildegard's literary-visual revelations is, once again, a fragmented life to say the least. As in Augustine and others, the largest fragments of Revelation to find a host in Hildegard are the climactic scenes of the resurrection of the dead, the Last Judgment, and the establishment of the reign of God in the new Jerusalem (Revelation 20–21). Yet, as we have seen, even these pieces are altered, revised, and rearranged in the course of their incorporation, "like one who mixes clay and then shapes it to any form he wishes" (3.11; recalling Jeremiah 18), Hildegard might say.

In fact, the tremendous popularity that Hildegard's own reanimation of Revelation in her *Scivias* enjoyed for centuries, and even now, owes a good deal to *its* fragmentability as well. Many who have revered it have not known it as a whole work of twenty-six visions in three books. Even Pope Eugenius III, who endorsed the work, thereby protecting Hildegard from censure by other authorities, did so based on reading an unfinished version that the highly influential monastic reformer and mystic Bernard of Clairvaux shared with him around 1147. And its growing influence over the next century was due in large part to the popularity of Cistercian prior Gebeno of Eberbach's *Pentacrhonon sive speculum futurorum temporum* [Five ages, or mirror of times to come], a small compilation of quotations from Hildegard's various works, including the *Scivias*, along with his own comments, published around 1220. This little book, along with many other works on or purportedly by Hildegard, had more to do with her spread and influence in the thirteenth century than the *Scivias* or any of her other complete works.[19]

Survival: *sur-vival*, "over-living" or "living beyond."[20] The survival of cultural works, living beyond their "original" lives in and through fragmentability, is by no means unique to Revelation and Hildegard. Still, we might wonder if apocalypses, especially those in the genealogy of Revelation, are particularly amenable to breaking up and spreading in this way. For one thing, apocalyptic visions in Christian tradition tend to be of particular *scenes* that can easily stand alone, apart from their larger narrative contexts. Beyond that, as we have seen, the images themselves, especially those of particular actors in the scenes, often both entice and defy the imagination. Examples from Revelation include "one like the Son of Man" with flaming eyes and a voice like many waters, winged singing creatures full of eyes all around and inside, and crowned locusts like horses with human faces. Examples from Hildegard include a physics-defying building of salvation, a bald-headed angry face with three huge wings, and a crowned woman with a monstrous face between her legs. Such figures often stick with us quite apart from others that are part of their scene, let alone their larger narrative context.

With Hildegard, moreover, the surviving and thriving of Revelation took on new, multimedia dimensions. There had been illuminated manuscripts of the book of Revelation itself before Hildegard's, including the eleventh-century *Bamberg Apocalypse*, which includes fifty-seven miniature illustrations along with the full Latin text of Revelation. But hers is a remarkable innovation that incorporates her own absorption of

Revelation along with many other scriptural traditions through her lifelong practice of *lectio divina* into a new form of apocalyptic imagination, an interaction between word and image in ways well beyond anything like biblical illustration.

Mind's Eye

Joachim in the Forests of History

Recall from the last chapter that it was a Cistercian prior named Gebeno of Eberbach who was largely responsible for popularizing Hildegard's prophecies through his little annotated compilation, *Pentacrhonon sive speculum futurorum temporum* [Five ages, or mirror of times to come], published around 1220. Part of the success of that booklet was that in it Gebeno drew associations between Hildegard's work and that of an already very well-known apocalyptic seer named Joachim of Fiore.

Joachim was nearly a contemporary of Hildegard. He was born around 1135 in the Calabria region of southern Italy (the mountainous and densely forested "toe" of the country's "foot"). He was expected to follow in his father's footsteps as a notary, but, after a trip to the Holy Land, he devoted himself to religious life, living in voluntary poverty as a hermit on Mount Etna and as an itinerant preacher in his hometown region. In 1171 he became a Benedictine monk at the monastery of Corazzo in the same region, and in 1177 he became its abbot, leading a campaign to incorporate it into the new order of the

Cistercians, a radical reform movement led by Bernard of Clairvaux that strove for stricter adherence to the Order of Saint Benedict.[1]

Even as Joachim was enmeshed in these administrative details, his mind was taking him into ever more complex contemplations of the mysterious meaning of the history of creation, from its beginnings to its final consummation. By 1192 these ideas would drive him and a group of followers out of the monastery at Corazzo to establish a new order, the Florensians, in the more austere climbs of the Calabrian mountains.

By the time of his death in 1202, Joachim was among the most well-known religious visionaries in Europe. In addition to many letters and treatises, he wrote three major books, *Exposition on the Apocalypse*, *The Book of Concordance*, and *The Ten-Stringed Psaltery,* all of which included elaborate visual illustrations. Most scholars now concur that he also created a fourth work that visually depicted his ideas, known as the *Liber Figurarum*, or *Book of Figures*.[2] Like Hildegard, Joachim was a picture thinker, incorporating depictions into his apocalyptic thinking throughout.

Exalted as a saint and true prophetic spirit by many, Joachim was condemned by others. After his death, his conception of the Trinity was denounced as heretical because some believed it leaned toward "tritheism" by treating Father, Son, and Holy Spirit as somewhat separate divine entities focused on different eras of history. He was included in the 1537 *Catalogus Haereticorum* [Catalog of Heretics] of Bernard of Luxembourg. Prominent theologians such as Thomas Aquinas and Bonaventure dismissed his prophecies as simple conjectures.[3] On the other hand, in Dante's *Paradiso*, Joachim "shines" among the saints alongside Bonaventure, who, despite his earthly criticisms, introduces him there as one endowed with a "spirit of prophecy."[4] Morever, his understanding of the Trinity clearly influenced later Catholic theology, especially in its emphasis on the developing roles of the different persons of the Trinity throughout history.

Saint or heretic, in the decades and centuries following his death, his ideas achieved tremendous influence and generated a veritable scholarly field of studies called Joachimism, in which explications, expansions, extrapolations, compilations, and visual redepictions of his apocalyptic ideas proliferated.

Unlike Hildegard, who explicitly claimed the mantle of prophecy, Joachim did not consider himself a prophet per se, but rather, as Bernard McGinn puts it, an "exegete to whom God had granted the gift of understanding the truth already revealed but hidden in the Bible."[5] His kind of apocalyptic spirituality was fundamentally hermeneutical, proceeding through literary and visual explication of the whole canon of Christian Scriptures as an intricately interrelated system to comprehend the entire time and space of the history of creation.

For Joachim, moreover, the book of Revelation was the hermeneutical key to understanding how every single part of Scripture operates in perfect harmony, or concordance, with every other. In his *Exposition on the Apocalypse*, he recalls this realization coming to him all at once, while he meditated in his "mind's eye" (*mentis oculis*) in the middle of the night. At once, he recalls, he "perceived a certain clarity of understanding" (*intelligentie claritate percepta*) about the completeness or "fullness of this book" (i.e., Revelation) and the "total concordance [*tota . . . concordantia*] between the Old and the New Testament."[6] For Joachim, Revelation revealed the total concordance of Scripture. It was the interpretive key to unlocking the signs, hidden throughout the Old and New Testaments, of divine will as it unfolded throughout the history of creation. What was ultimately revealed was the knowledge that he and his followers stood at the very edge of the world as they knew it. The end was near, very near, and the need to prepare the way of the Lord was urgent.

Forests of Histories

In Joachim's apocalyptic imagination, biblical texts are often read backward and forward in relation with one another. Thus, for example, he reads the early Christian text of Revelation as the hermeneutical key to understanding the Hebrew prophet Ezekiel's vision of the four-winged creatures and the wheel inside the wheel (Ezekiel 1). Joachim decodes this vision as a way into what he calls the "forests of histories" in the Old and New Testaments. First, here is Ezekiel's vision:

> Each [of the four creatures] had four faces, and each of them had four wings. . . . And the four had their

faces and their wings thus: their wings touched one another; each of them moved straight ahead, without turning as they moved. . . . The four had the face of a human being, the face of a lion on the right side, the face of an ox on the left side, and the face of an eagle. . . . As I looked at the living creatures, I saw a wheel on the earth beside the living creatures, one for each of the four of them. . . . The four had the same form, their construction being something like a wheel within a wheel. When they moved, they moved in any of the four directions without veering as they moved. Their rims were tall and awesome, for the rims of all four were full of eyes all round. When the living creatures moved, the wheels moved beside them . . . for the spirit of the living creatures was in the wheels. (Ezekiel 1:6–20)

Ezekiel describes four interconnected creatures with four different animal faces hovering in the heavens. Each heavenly creature moves in sync with a pair of earthly wheels, one inside the other. And each animal-plus-wheels set moves in a kind of synchronized dance, in which the pairs of wheels on earth shadow the movements of their corresponding heavenly creatures.[7]

Joachim finds in this vision a diagram for understanding what he calls "all of the forests of histories which overshadow the Old Testament."[8] These forests of histories, he explains, include five histories, one general history and four particular histories. "For," he writes, "there is one wheel, having four faces. There is one general history to which four special [histories] are joined." Thus, it appears that Joachim reads the four wheels within wheels as all being in some sense essentially the same wheel, which is connected to the four faces of the four creatures.

The general history, which corresponds to the outer wheels in Ezekiel's vision, is "that which proceeds from the beginning of the world straight through the book of Ezra," that is, the large narrative arc of biblical history from creation in Genesis 1 to the return of the Judean people from Babylonian exile and their rebuilding of the Jerusalem temple in Ezra and Nehemiah. The four faces, then, are four specific or "little" biblical histories, namely, the stories of Job, Esther, and the apocryphal stories of Tobit and Judith, that take place outside that larger historical arc. "That is the wheel, these the faces," but that is not the only concordance with these four faces, nor with the wheel. For these elements also relate to the forest of the history of the New Testament. With respect to that testament, Joachim continues, the four particular faces are the four Gospels of Matthew, Mark, Luke, and John. And what of Revelation? It is in fact the wheel *inside* the outer wheel of general history.

In this light, the book of Revelation is both a timeline and a microcosm of the broad, overarching history of creation. As such, in Joachim's imagination, biblical history, which encompasses everything, is both *diachronic* and *synchronic*: it is a linear story of God's plan for the world that proceeds through time (diachronic) from creation to culmination; at the same time, it is also a kind of multilayered map, like a geographical information system (GIS), which, for those with eyes to see, becomes a means of uncovering and deciphering the hidden spatial (synchronic) geography of history, in which past, present, and future interact with and mirror one another. Thus, the total will of God for creation, which is easily missed in its densely forested manifestation, both in everyday experience and in the details of the Old and New Testaments, is revealed in the Apocalypse of John, the microcosmic wheel within the cosmic wheel of general history. Revelation is its concordance, index, and interpretive key.

Joachim then breaks down the entire text of Revelation itself into eight historical eras of the Christian church: the opening and letters to the seven churches (Revelation 1:1–3:22); the seven seals (4:1–8:1); the seven trumpets (8:2–12:18, which includes cosmic destruction, plagues, the locusts, the two witnesses, the woman clothed with the sun, and the red dragon); the two beasts (13:1–14:20); the seven bowls of plagues (14:21–16:21); the destruction of Babylon and the beasts (17:1–19:21); the new millennium of Christ's reign, including the binding and later defeat of the dragon as well as the Last Judgment (20:1–15); and the new heaven, new earth, and new Jerusalem (21:1–22:21). Of these eras, the first seven, which he also conceives as the seven "days" of the "final week," correspond to the seven eras of Church history that begin with the New Testament. The eighth corresponds to the culmination of creation and the end of history in the eternal reign of God with the saints.

Red Dragon

Revelation, then, not only encodes and, with Joachim's solicitation, reveals the shape of general cosmic history from creation to consummation. It also gives its own more specific history of the Church and where "we," that is, Joachim and his followers, stand within it—namely, in the last days.

But the correspondences do not end here. Joachim finds in particular images from Revelation still more specific, microcosmic sets of historical sevens *within* these seven major eras of the Church, which are themselves set within the larger wheel of the history of creation. The seven seals opened by seven angels in what Joachim identifies as the second part of Revelation also represent the seven eras of the Church *as well as* the seven eras of Old Testament history.

Among all these sevens within sevens, the seven heads of the red dragon in Revelation 12 (part of what Joachim identifies as the third major part of Revelation) take on particular significance and influence. This particular interpretation owes its popularity not only to Joachim's extensive written commentary on the text but also to the highly compelling color illustration, that is, the interacting word and image that he created in his *Book of Figures* to explicate and expand upon his words.[9]

The medium of the large folio manuscript codex was especially amenable to Joachim's work, especially his *Book of Figures*, in a way that later print book media would not have been. Printing press technology requires a fixed layout of set and locked metal type that is of

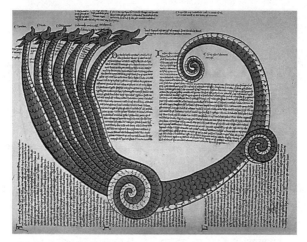

FIGURE 5.1. Joachim of Fiore, illustration of the Great Dragon, *Liber Figurarum*; Reggio Emilia Codex, Library of the Seminary of Reggio Emilia, mid-thirteenth century.

uniform size, line length, margins, and so on, with images set apart from text on part or all of a page. By contrast, in the calligraphic mode of manuscript book art, images as well as words, lines, and larger bodies of handwritten text in various sizes and colors can bend around images, cut across and between them, and interact with them and other texts in ways that resist linear reading strategies while producing complex spatial relationships between different elements.

Joachim's figure of the red dragon is an excellent illustration of the effects that are possible in such a medium. The dragon itself runs across a full folio of parchment. Its seven heads reach on long, scaly necks across the upper left-hand side of the sheet, while its thick torso curls down across the bottom of the sheet before turning up into the curly tail found in the upper right-hand corner. All around the dragon's body are handwritten lines of text, mostly in black ink but sometimes in red. Words and phrases lace the dragon's heads, while larger blocks of commentary fill the spaces around the body. The various pieces of text are laid out in different directions on the page so that one needs to keep turning it clockwise and counterclockwise to read it. These different bodies of text, moreover, are not presented in any particular sequence that would require one to read from one section to the next; rather, it is up to the reader, or rather the user, to decide where to start and how to proceed.[10] It is a truly interactive work of manuscript media.

The red dragon of Revelation 12, which is Joachim's inspiration for this figure, possesses its own complex genealogy. As I have argued elsewhere, it inherits features from a range of Hebrew biblical chaos monsters, especially the "sea monster" and Leviathan, which is a chaos monster that is sometimes identified with and glorified by God (e.g., Job 41 and Psalm 104) and other times set against God as creation's worst enemy.[11] In Joachim's work, that genealogy is not so much sorted out as further complexified. For the red dragon is not simply a figure of Satan; rather, it is an embodiment of the whole history of the Church's trials and tribulations, past, present, and future.

"The seven heads of the dragon," Joachim explains in script that curves gracefully around the painting of the red dragon itself, "signify seven tyrants by whom the persecutions of the Church were begun."[12] Above each of the heads is the name of the persecutor, and along each neck are details about the population responsible for the persecutions and how, by their persecutions, they purified and strengthened the Church (these seven also concord with the seven persecutions of Israel in the Old Testament). Five heads are identified with persecutions that have already taken place: the persecution of the Jews, led by King Herod during the time of the Apostles; the persecution of the Pagans, led by the Roman Emperor Nero during the time of the Martyrs; the persecution of the Heretics, led by the Arian Emperor Constantius II during the time of the Doctors (i.e., the fathers of Church orthodoxy); the persecution of the Saracens, or Arab Muslims, led by Mohammed during the time of the Virgins; and the persecution of the "sons of Babylon," led by Mesemoth (probably a north African Moorish ruler) during the time of the Conventuals (Franciscan clerics who, in opposition to the more radical Spirituals, accommodated other orders and were agreeable with the will of the papacy).[13]

These persecutions are all in the past. The sixth head, which wears a crown, represents a persecution that is both already underway *and* soon to come. The head itself, Joachim says, is Saladin, that is, Salah ad-Din Yusuf ibn Ayyub (1137–93), the first sultan of Syria and Egypt and the founding ruler of the Sunni Muslim Ayyubid dynasty. In 1169 Saladin had taken control of Egypt and begun establishing an empire throughout the Middle East. By 1183 he had captured the major Syrian cities of Damascus and Aleppo, and in 1187 he defeated the

Christian Crusaders and took control of Palestine, including Jerusalem.

Noting that the dragon of Revelation has seven heads *and ten horns* (12:3), Joachim explains that the ten horns are actually all on this sixth head, because this king will gather under him the ten other kings mentioned later in Revelation, who will "receive authority as kings for one hour, together with the beast" in order to wage war against Christ before they, along with the beast, are ultimately conquered (Revelation 17:12–15). At first, Joachim explains, Saladin will rule alone. Soon, however, either he will be raised from the dead or his immediate successor will rise up and gather these other kings under him, at which time the persecutions of the Church will increase greatly, inciting "universal war against God's elect. Many will be crowned with martyrdom in those days."[14]

Before the end of this universal persecution by the sixth head and his ten horns, the dragon's seventh head, which represents the Antichrist himself, will rise up. Recall that this false messiah, often identified with the beast of Revelation, is expected to presage the Second Coming and Last Judgment, persecuting believers and deluding the masses into worshipping him. The dragon's last two heads will be joined in a "twin tribulation" of Christians around the world. In this sense, Joachim writes, the sixth and seventh persecutions of the Church will take place together during the era of the sixth of seven seals, rather than during the time of the seventh seal, which, as mentioned previously, will be the era of the millennial reign of Christ, when "the dragon's heads will be crushed and he will be imprisoned in the abyss"—an image that combines the description in Revelation of the dragon chained in the abyss (20:2) and the description in Psalm 74 of God crushing the heads of the dragon Leviathan (74:13–14). As such, the heads/kings/tribulations are seven in number but "are destined to be fulfilled under the one sixth time" of the "final week."

The tail of the dragon, however, is also the Antichrist. Although the dragon's heads will be crushed at the beginning of Christ's millennial reign, the dragon will not be defeated once and for all until the end of that millennium, after being released for a short time. The caption on the tail reads, "Gog. He is the Final Antichrist." So Gog, who, along with Magog, represents the Devil's armies defeated by God in the final battle of Revelation (20:8), is in Joachim's schema yet another Antichrist.

The body of the dragon, which nearly forms a full circle as it curves from the seventh head to the tail through the written words of commentary is that millennium, or "Sabbath age." It is *also* the abyss in which the dragon will be imprisoned and from which it will be released for a time before its final destruction and the coming of the eighth era, that is, the coming of the new heaven, the new earth, and the new Jerusalem (Revelation 21:2).[15]

So the red dragon comes to embody the history of the church as a history of tribulations which, one by one, prepare the church for the coming reign of Christ, when that same diabolical serpent's body will be destroyed. In a sense, then, the dragon is not simply God's and the Church's archenemy but is also part of the divine plan, its tribulations essential for the purification of the people of God and its very body mapping the way to ultimate redemption.

Alpha and Omega

Joachim's literary-visual figurings of Scripture as encoded history are intricately structured and multi-layered. Particular units fall into patterns that concord with larger parallel patterns which concord with still larger ones, until nearly every detail of the Old and New Testaments seems to have found its place within his system.

As Marjorie Reeves and Beatrice Hirsch-Reich emphasize, Joachim is by no means a systematician. On the contrary,

> there is a kaleidoscopic quality about his mind which sets [different elements] moving in ever-changing patterns. He does not deal with concepts in orderly succession and we have to catch the shifting designs of his imagination. As he writes, the images constantly arrange and rearrange themselves, as in a rich and complex dance, and Joachim himself is conscious of bewilderment at the intricacies of the figures which move before his mind's eye.[16]

Joachim is not simply about building a framework in order to comprehend every theological element—God, creation, human nature, sin, redemption, and so on—within a total and totalizing system of meaning. The patterns he sees are less structural than they are fractal. Within his apocalyptic imagination, everything relates to everything else through the shape of its meaning; larger units comprise smaller units of the same structure and pattern, and vice versa.

We would be mistaken, therefore, to expect his different visual figures to integrate entirely into one another. Compare, for example, the figure of the red dragon with another of his figures, that of the trinitarian circles. There, instead of the patterns of sevens we have seen so far, we find threes: three overlapping circles, each simultaneously representing one of the persons of the Trinity, a period in the biblical history of creation, and that period's social "order."

The first circle, identified with the person of God the Father, encompasses the period from Adam to Christ, which was the order of "the married," that is, the ancestral lineage that leads to Christ. The second circle, identified with the person of God the Son, encompasses the period from King Josiah, the reformer of the Southern Kingdom of Judah (2 Kings 22–23; whose labors began to bear fruit with Christ), to Joachim's present time. This period was the order of the "clerics," or members of clergy. And the third circle, identified with the person of the Holy Spirit, encompasses the period of the New Testament, especially from the Order of Saint Benedict to the end of the world, that is, to the total fulfillment of creation and union with the divine, which means the end of the Church. It represents the order of monasticism, which for Joachim is the most spiritually evolved

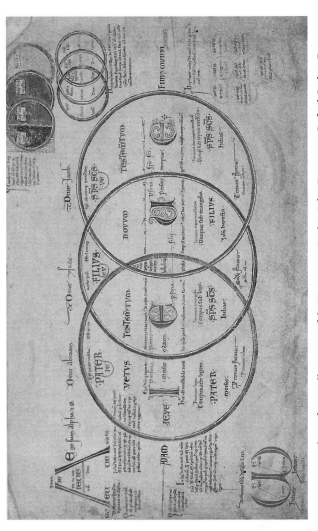

FIGURE 5.2. Joachim of Fiore, illustration of the Trinitarian Circles, *Liber Figurarum*, Oxford Codex, Corpus Christi College, early thirteenth century.

social order, necessary to realize the culmination of history in union with God.

Although it may not be obvious on first view, Revelation, or rather one very small bit of it, is as central to this figure as it was to that of the red dragon. That bit is God's self-declaration in Revelation: "I am the Alpha and the Omega . . . who is and who was and who is to come, the almighty" (1:8; cf. 21:6, 22:13; Joachim's Latin quotation is, "*Ego sum Alpha & Omega principiu & finis dicit dominus deus qui est & qui erat et qui uenturus est omnipotens*"). Through both literary and visual means, Joachim ties this naming of God to the three circles of the Trinity, the historical periods they encircle, *and* the Tetragrammaton, יהוה (read right to left, *yod-hey-vav-hey*, commonly transliterated "Yʜᴡʜ"), which is the Hebrew proper name for the biblical God. In the process of making these associations, Joachim makes from this naming of God in Revelation as Alpha and Omega an image of the total unity of the divine as the ground of all history.[17]

On the upper left-hand side of the folio is a large blue uppercase Greek letter Alpha (A) whose triangular shape and three points represent the three-in-oneness of the Trinity as an image of both unity and difference. At the topmost point is the word "*Pater*" ("Father"), at the lower left point is the word "*Filius*" ("Son"), and at the lower right point is the word "*Spiritus Sanctus*" ("Holy Spirit"). Linked to each of these three corners and persons of the Trinity is a pair of letters from Joachim's transliteration of the Hebrew Tetragrammaton, "IEUE" (I for the Hebrew letter *yod*, E for *hey*, and U for *vav*). Thus "*Pater*" is linked to the first two letters, "IE"; "*Filius*" is linked to the middle two letters, "EU"; and "*Spiritus Sanctus*" is linked to the last two letters, "UE." Then, in the center of the Alpha is written "*Trinitas*," "IEUE," and "*unus Deus*" ("unity of God"). Thus, the three persons of the Trinity come to contain the Hebrew divine name even as they interlock with one another through overlapping letters, again conveying both unity and difference, all within the letter and image of Alpha.

In the lower left-hand corner of the folio, directly below the Alpha, is the other half of the divine epithet given in Revelation, a large, red, lowercase Omega (ω). Here, too, we find inscribed both the persons of the Trinity and the letters of the Tetragrammaton, but in a different arrangement: "I" and "Father" are in the lower left bowl of the letter; "U" and "Son" are in the lower right bowl; and "E" and "Holy Spirit" are in both in the openings at the top. So, reading from bottom to top and left to right, from Father to Spirit to Son to Spirit, we once again find the sequence I-E-U-E.

To the right of the large figures of the Alpha and Omega, the Omega (ω) is replaced, without explanation, by the Greek letter Omicron (O), that is, a circle, or rather many circles.[18] It first appears as a small circle containing the letters of the Tetragrammaton, and then as three larger overlapping circles representing the Trinity, each of which contains the associated pairs of letters from the Tetragrammaton that appeared in the Alpha (IE with the Father, EU with the Son, and UE with the Holy Spirit). Recall, moreover, each large circle also represents a major period in the history of creation, from beginning to end, Alpha to Omega, what "was, is, and is to come" (Revelation 1:8). Thus, here again, Revelation comes to represent and embody the totality of God and history.

You Are Here

As complex and multilayered as Joachim's visual-textual diagrams of interrelated letters, triangles, circles, sevens within sevens, and wheels within wheels are, part of what made his work so compelling to so many was the fact that all of its details were tied to specific historical events. Indeed, according to his elaborate scriptural accountings and mappings, all of history appeared to be leading to his present time. Imagine, on the one hand, being overwhelmed by all the interconnected visual and textual detail in this map of divine creation and, on the other hand, being told "you are here" within it. You are located and oriented within a world that is at the same time profoundly disorienting.

The great irony of the book of Revelation, as we have seen, is that what it claims to reveal remains very much hidden, behind the veil, encrypted and encoded within and between its lines. It is an apocalypse (*apo-kalupto*, "from covering") that covers more than it uncovers, a revelation (*re-velare*, "unveiling") that veils more than it unveils. It uncovers a covering, reveals a veiling.

One of Joachim's favorite biblical images comes from the story of Moses's veiled face (Exodus 34:29–35). When Moses came down from Mount Sinai with the tablets of the law, his face was so radiant with divine presence that it terrified the Israelites. Therefore, whenever he was not addressing them, he would cover his face with a veil (Latin Vulgate *velum*, related to *revelare*).[19] This same veil is referred to metaphorically in Paul's second letter to the Corinthians, where he writes, "When one turns to the Lord, the veil is removed," and "all of us, with unveiled faces," now behold God's glory "as though reflected in a mirror" (2 Corinthians 3:16–18).[20] In Joachim's work, the veiled texts of Scripture are brought to light via the kaleidoscopic play of mirrors, revealing to the "mind's eye" shapes and patterns heretofore hidden. And Revelation is the key to everything.

In digital media technology, a "codec" is a device or program that both encodes and decodes information (the term itself is a portmanteau of the words "code" and "decode"). Early codecs were hardware devices such as CD and DVD recorders and players that encoded analog data into digital form for storage, and then decoded that data back into analog form for users to access. Later the term was adopted for computer programs, especially video and audio codecs like QuickTime and MPEG, which encode and compress sounds and images for digital storage and decode them for viewing and listening.

In Joachim's hands, Revelation was something like a medieval codec, a device for both encoding and decoding information about the past, present, and future of sacred history. Those with eyes to see could discover that information encoded and stored within it, and then watch as it decoded itself, in the clear understanding of his "mind's eye," into the full meaning of the entirety of sacred history. Thus, Joachim brought Revelation to life in yet another new form, as a kind of codec in which is encoded the full truth of the entirety of Scriptures, which themselves embody and comprehend the entirety of God's plan for creation from beginning to end. Its scenes and images are decoded to reveal actual historical events and persons along that larger biblical arc.

As rigorously analytical as it is creatively imaginative, this apocalyptic methodology is intensely visual, spinning itself out in lavish designs wherein shapes and patterns mirror letters and words and vice-versa. Indeed, unlike Hildegard's images, which are for the most part representational, depicting particular apocalyptic scenes that involve recognizable if also often disturbingly unusual characters, Joachim's visual figures are built from abstractions: shapes become letters and words, even as letters and words become shapes, touching and overlapping to create interconnected webs of space and time, revealing the mind of God to the mind's eye of the seer.

While Joachim's particular biblical interpretations have been highly influential since even before his death, his creatively intellectual apocalyptic *methodology* of visual figuring in word and image has proven even more influential. We will see its lineage running through the subsequent life of Revelation, flourishing especially in the visual diagrams of late nineteenth- and early twentieth-century interpreters like Clarence Larkin (1850–1924), whose visual designs of sacred history as a series of dispensations of divine grace have been cornerstones of

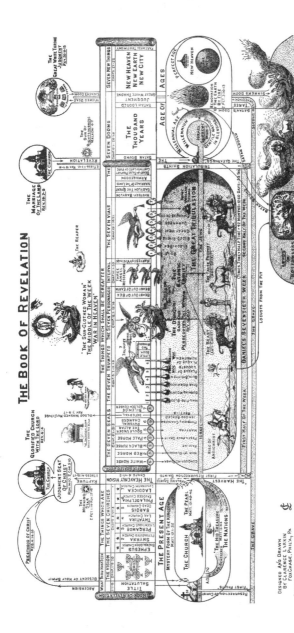

FIGURE 5.3: Clarence Larkin, diagram of historical dispensations as deciphered from the book of Revelation, *Dispensational Truth*, 1918.

Christian fundamentalism. The Joachimite ancestry of such visual dispensationalism is unmistakable.[21]

Not surprisingly, for Joachim as for the hosts who have followed him in this approach, the maps and diagrams always seem to reveal the present moment as most significant. You are here, they show us, on the very cusp of God's favored time, at the very beginning of escalation toward the consummation of all things, which is just around the corner. What a radical departure from Augustine's *City of God*, which pushed Revelation's seals, trumpets, and beasts well into the distant future. From now on, the end is near.

September's Testament

Luther's Bible vs. Cranach's Revelation

CHAPTER 6

Recall that the book of Revelation was far from a shoo-in for inclusion in the canon of the New Testament during the early centuries of Christianity. Its case was strengthened by those who confused its John with John the beloved disciple, to whom was attributed the Gospel of John and the three letters of John. Still, many rejected it, calling it an incoherent, poorly conceived, and badly written fraud. Well into the fourth century, as Eusebius makes clear, its scriptural status was a matter of dispute. Yes, Bishop Athanasius does include it as the final book of his New Testament canon in 367 CE, but the fact that he needed to assert this particular canonical list in the first place suggests that what was in and what was out was still a matter of disagreement.

Recall, too, that the establishment of the New Testament canon by the end of the fourth century had as much to do with media technology as it did with ecclesiastical authority. The establishment of Roman Christianity as the religion of the empire, which led to an increasing drive to consolidate and control ecclesiastical power, coincided with the development of the media technology of a codex big enough to hold an entire canon of Old and New Testament texts in a single volume. The new medium of the big codex and the new status of Christendom as imperial religion worked hand in hand to close the canon.

By 420 CE, Jerome had produced an entire Bible in the Latin of his time, based primarily on translations of Greek and Hebrew biblical texts. This Bible, which included the same twenty-seven books of the New Testament as Athanasius's list, eventually became the standard Vulgate Bible for all of Western Christianity.

Yet we would be mistaken to believe that this closing of the canon was entirely secure or permanent. Indeed, the Vulgate itself was never fixed nor changeless. Although Jerome had excluded books such as Baruch and Tobit as apocryphal because they did not appear in his Hebrew manuscripts, all the Vulgate Bibles that have survived include them. And although he, like Athanasius, had excluded Paul's letter to the Laodiceans, some of the oldest known manuscripts of the Vulgate include it. Another early manuscript replaces the four separate Gospels with a single harmonization.[1]

We might have expected the invention in the fifteenth century of the printing press and the rise of print book culture, with the Bible as its flagship, to have finally fixed and closed the biblical canon once and for all. Mechanical printing and fixed type, after all, made it possible to produce thousands of copies of one book, each identical to the next. But for such biblical uniformity and permanence to be achieved, there would need to have been a single, original book to mass-produce in the first place. When it came to Christian Scriptures, there was no such thing. What happened with the print revolution, then, was not a fixing and binding of the Bible, but a greater unfixing and unbinding of it.[2] Within two decades of the publication of Gutenberg's first Latin Vulgate Bible in 1456, there were nine German Bibles in print. By the mid-sixteenth century, as Protestantism gained momentum, many different Bibles would appear in many other modern languages as well, and these would often include different canons of different texts translated from different "original" manuscripts in Latin, Greek, and Hebrew.

In fact, the Protestant Reformation was as much a media revolution as it was a theological revolution. It was in many respects a biblical-literacy movement, aimed at making the Bible as readily available and accessible as possible in order to make real the ideal of a "priesthood of all believers." At the same time, print culture was quickly transforming Bibles and other books from collectable manuscripts into tradable commodities. They were no longer held strictly within the domain of wealthy and powerful patrons who commissioned expensive hand copies of whole Vulgate Bibles, Gospel Books, and Psalmodies for churches, monasteries, and the homes of the literate elites. It was a nightmare of democratization that the Roman Church of the fourth century could never have imagined.

There Are Many Far Better Books

Here is where Revelation comes back into the picture, and its scriptural status back into question. Its embrace by Church authorities like Athanasius and theologians like Augustine in the fourth and fifth centuries had not fully guaranteed its continued inclusion as canonical within the new media revolution of the Protestant Reformation.

On September 21, 1522, Martin Luther published his German translation of the New Testament in his hometown of Wittenberg, Germany.[3] Known as the "September Testament," it was a landmark in the history of printing, the German language, and the Christian Bible. The first translation of the New Testament into modern vernacular language, Luther's text used the eastern and central German dialect, which helped establish it as the standard for the High German to follow. His decision to base his translation on Erasmus's edition of the Greek New Testament, moreover, presented a not-so-subtle challenge to Roman Catholic tradition, which insisted on the Latin Vulgate as the only authoritative text. Erasmus's edition had two columns per page: the beautifully type-designed Greek printed on the inside column, and Erasmus's own Latin translation of that text on the outside column. Given that his translation frequently diverged significantly from the Vulgate, this text was an implicit questioning of the reliability and authority of the Vulgate text, a fact that would not have been missed by Luther.

But Luther's challenge to the authority of the Roman Church went deeper still, reopening the question of which books should be included in the Christian canon of the emerging Reformation movement. This is clear even in the September Testament's table of contents page: although it lists all twenty-seven books of the traditional Catholic canon, it numbers only the first twenty-three, which are attributed to saints. The last four books— "The Epistle to the Hebrews," "The Epistle of James," "The Epistle of Jude," "The Revelation of John"—are left unnumbered and set apart by extra spaces at the bottom of the page.

The canonical challenge of the September Testament is clearest, however, in Luther's prefatory comments to the different books, especially Revelation. There he writes,

> About this Book of the Revelation of John, I leave everyone free to hold his own opinions. I would not have anyone bound to my opinion or judgment. I say what I feel. I miss more than one thing in this book, and it makes me consider it to be neither apostolic nor prophetic.[4]

Noting that some church fathers also rejected the book, he writes that he sees no evidence of the Holy Spirit in it, complaining that, unlike the apostles, it does not speak plainly but deals "exclusively with visions and images" that are left uninterpreted. Referring to John's claims to authority in the last chapter of Revelation, Luther continues,

> Moreover he [John] seems to me to be going much too far when he commends his own book so highly [22:6, 16]—indeed, more than any of the other sacred

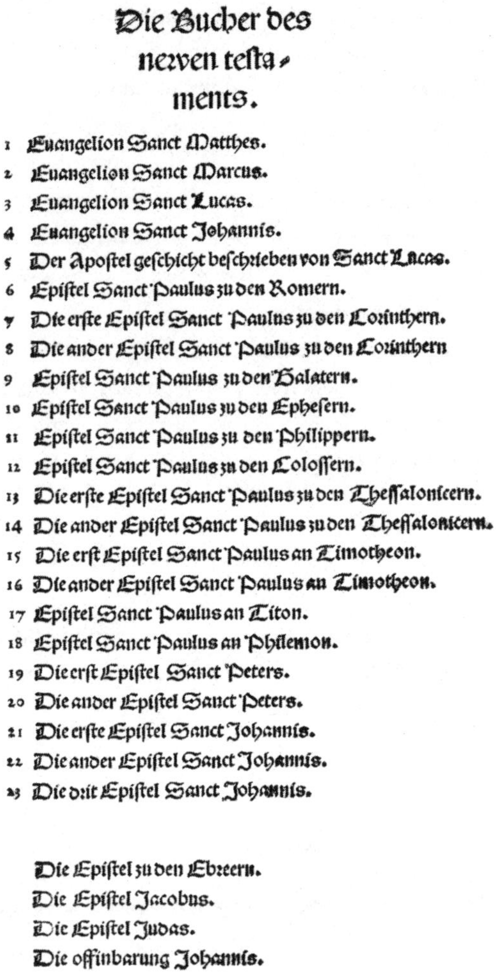

Die Bucher des newen testaments.

1 Euangelion Sanct Matthes.
2 Euangelion Sanct Marcus.
3 Euangelion Sanct Lucas.
4 Euangelion Sanct Johannis.
5 Der Apoſtel geſchicht beſchrieben von Sanct Lucas.
6 Epiſtel Sanct Paulus zu den Romern.
7 Die erſte Epiſtel Sanct Paulus zu den Corinthern.
8 Die ander Epiſtel Sanct Paulus zu den Corinthern
9 Epiſtel Sanct Paulus zu den Galatern.
10 Epiſtel Sanct Paulus zu den Epheſern.
11 Epiſtel Sanct Paulus zu den Philippern.
12 Epiſtel Sanct Paulus zu den Coloſſern.
13 Die erſte Epiſtel Sanct Paulus zu den Theſſalonicern.
14 Die ander Epiſtel Sanct Paulus zu den Theſſalonicern.
15 Die erſt Epiſtel Sanct Paulus an Timotheon.
16 Die ander Epiſtel Sanct Paulus an Timotheon.
17 Epiſtel Sanct Paulus an Titon.
18 Epiſtel Sanct Paulus an Philemon.
19 Die erſt Epiſtel Sanct Peters.
20 Die ander Epiſtel Sanct Peters.
21 Die erſte Epiſtel Sanct Johannis.
22 Die ander Epiſtel Sanct Johannis.
23 Die dritt Epiſtel Sanct Johannis.

Die Epiſtel zu den Ebreern.
Die Epiſtel Jacobus.
Die Epiſtel Judas.
Die offinbarung Johannis.

FIGURE. 6.1. Table of contents page from Luther's September Testament, 1522. Image provided courtesy of the Richard C. Kessler Reformation Collection, Pitts Theology Library, Candler School of Theology, Emory University.

books do, though they are much more important. . . . Again, they are supposed to be blessed who keep what is written in this book [22:7, 9]; and yet no one knows what that is, to say nothing of keeping it. This is just the same as if we did not have the book at all. And there are many far better books available for us to keep.

Go with your gut, Luther says, in so many words. "I say what I feel," and so should you. He concludes, "My spirit cannot accommodate itself to this book." That, he writes, is reason enough to leave it behind and "stick to the books which present Christ to me clearly and purely."

Luther had no interest in drawing anyone's attention to Revelation. Indeed, he clearly meant to steer readers away from it. Yet quite the opposite happened, thanks to the inclusion of twenty-one stunning full-page woodcut illustrations of scenes from Revelation by his friend and colleague, Lucas Cranach the Elder. Whereas Luther would have buried Revelation once and for all, Cranach's images in Luther's Bible gave Revelation new life, not as literary text but as an overwhelming visual encounter.

Supernatural

Lucas Cranach the Elder (1472–1553) was the court painter in Wittenberg for Frederick the Wise, Elector of Saxony from 1504 to 1550. He was also a member of City Council and a successful businessman, running an apothecary, trading in paper, and owning a printing shop, among other ventures. At one point he was the largest private landowner in Wittenberg. But Cranach is best known today for his longtime partnership with his close friend Martin Luther. In addition to his illustrations for the September Testament and later the Luther Bible, he published many early Protestant writings and painted the official marriage portrait of Martin and Katharina Luther, as well as of Martin's parents. His own biblical paintings, moreover, reflect Luther's strong theological influence, especially his insistence on justification by faith alone—the belief that one is saved not by devotion, good works, or even right doctrine but only by the grace freely given by God through Christ.[5]

Earlier German Bibles printed in Cologne and Nuremberg had included illustrations of biblical scenes, especially from the Old Testament.[6] Luther was initially opposed to including illustrations in Bibles, because he worried they would distract readers and hearers from the written word. But he had changed his mind by the time he published his own first Bible, the September Testament—at least to a degree. It has historiated initials (large initial letters decorated with imagery from the story told in the text) for each of the New Testament books, but it only includes actual illustrations of biblical scenes for the book he finds most repellent, Revelation, apparently on account of the literary inscrutability that he complains about in his preface.

Most of Cranach's illustrations were based on and adapted from Albrecht Dürer's fifteen full-page woodcut illustrations in his print book edition of Revelation,

Apocalypsis cum figuris (*Revelation with Pictures*). First published in Nuremberg in 1498, two years before many believed the Last Judgment would commence, Dürer's illustrated book of Revelation was popular and well regarded, demonstrating the potential for producing richly complex and expressive artwork in the new medium of the print book. Departing from earlier colored illustrations of Bible scenes, his groundbreaking black-and-while images were highly complex, richly detailed, and emotionally evocative. Much of their effect was the result of what art historian Erwin Panofsky describes as Dürer's paradoxical rendering of supernatural subjects in naturalistic ways.[7] In so doing, we might say that his images naturalized the supernatural even as they supernaturalized the natural. Such an effect both responds to and intensifies another dynamic we have seen running through the lives of Revelation: how its literary descriptions both compel and defy visual depiction.

Of Cranach's twenty-one illustrations—nearly one per chapter—thirteen draw from those of Dürer.[8] The influence on those images is clearly not only in Cranach's general arrangement of figures within each landscape but also in the way disorienting energy is created through overcrowded scenes and through the prevalence of curving lines whirling around and emanating from different divine, human, and monstrous characters.

At the same time, Cranach departs from his precursor in highly significant ways. Not only does he intentionally simplify the illustrations, reducing the number of characters and elements in his scenes (e.g., separating Dürer's illustration of both the fifth and sixth seals into two separate illustrations) but he also alters particular details to conform more fully to the literal details of Luther's text. Thus, for example, whereas Dürer has John kneel reverently in prayer before the vision of the risen Christ as "one like the Son of Man" (Revelation 1:12–17), Cranach has him lying face down on the ground, since the text (Luther's as well as that in other editions) describes him falling down at his feet "as though dead" (1:17).

But what most powerfully distinguishes Cranach from Dürer in his depictions of Revelation is his rendering of the supernatural. Whereas Dürer naturalized his supernatural subjects, rendering divine beings and diabolical monsters alike into the familiar forms and proportions of humans and animals, Cranach made them weird, rendering such figures—especially the diabolical ones—as supernaturally and unnaturally *strange*.

Power in their Heads and Tails

Consider, for example, Cranach's and Dürer's depictions of the release of the four angels of death from the Euphrates to lead a cavalry that will slaughter a third of all humankind.

Here is the description in the book of Revelation:

So the four angels were released, who had been held ready for the hour, the day, the month, and the year, to kill a third of humankind. The number of the

FIGURE 6.2. Albrecht Dürer, woodcut illustration of the sixth trumpet, *Apocalypsis cum figuris*, 1498. Courtesy of the Wetmore Print Collection, Connecticut College.

FIGURE 6.3. Lucas Cranach the Elder, woodcut illustration of the sixth trumpet (Revelation 9:15–19) in Luther's September Testament, 1522. Image provided courtesy of the Richard C. Kessler Reformation Collection, Pitts Theology Library, Candler School of Theology, Emory University.

troops of cavalry was two hundred million; I heard their number. And this was how I saw the horses in my vision: the riders wore breastplates the color of fire and of sapphire and of sulfur; the heads of the horses were like lions' heads, and fire and smoke and sulfur came out of their mouths. By these three plagues a third of humankind was killed, by the fire and smoke and sulfur coming out of their mouths. For the power of the horses is in their mouths and in their tails; their tails are like serpents, having heads; and with them they inflict harm. (9:15–19)

Cranach's woodcut clearly follows Dürer's in its general layout and framing. In both images, a bearded and robed God sits enthroned behind an altar in the heavens with rays emanating from his head; he is flanked by two angels, with the one on the right blowing the sixth trumpet to release the angels of death and their cavalry; the heavens are encircled by clouds, separating that space from the one below, where masses of people are being slain by four-winged, sword-wielding angels as the cavalry arrives on the scene. Also in both images, the details of parallel curving and straight lines fill the space of the battle below with motion and energy, in contrast to the orderly, relatively static, cloud-encircled space of the heavens above, where the figures are arranged symmetrically. Thus, although Cranach's woodcut is far less detailed and textured than Dürer's, his basic layout and arrangement of the main characters and other objects is very similar.

Yet Cranach's illustration departs dramatically from Dürer's in its rendering of supernatural figures, especially the horses of the cavalry. In Dürer's woodcut, the horses appear in the background, emerging from the clouds to join the angels in battle. Their heads are naturally lion-like, their tails look more horse-like than serpent-like, and their sizes and proportions are natural and normal. From a distance, they simply look like horses.

In Cranach's woodcut, by contrast, everything is weirdly, supernaturally chaotic. The horses are front and center, in the middle of the page and the battle, trampling humans underhoof and nearly bowling over their angelic commanders. Their heads are oddly shaped and slightly out of perspective, as though appearing in a funhouse mirror. Most strikingly, their tails are huge, twisting serpents, as long as the horses themselves, with sharp, pointy tongues stretching from their open mouths. The horse-likeness of these figures is overwhelmed by their monstrously unhorselike heads and tails. John's words might well serve as a caption for Cranach's image: "The power of the horses is in their mouths and in their tails" (9:19).

The battle scene itself is also more chaotic in Cranach's depiction than in Dürer's, creating a greater sense of disorientation and instability. The bodies of people and angels tilt and lean in all directions as the horses plow through, their snake tails writhing and curling above the fray, mirroring the weirdly unnatural, intestine-like tube of cloud that separates them from the heavens. And look: there are five snake tails but only four horses visible.

At the same time, all this unnatural mess down below stands in sharp contrast against the rather dully ordered scene up in heaven, with an immobile God enthroned in the simple symmetry of straight lines, right angles, and empty white space, thereby encouraging the viewer's attention to focus on the violence and chaos down below.

Cranach's attention to the supernatural monstrosity of Revelation's scenes is even more striking in his illustrations that are *not* based on Dürer's. Among the most overwhelming is his depiction of the fifth trumpet, which opens the bottomless pit and summons forth locust-like fiends to torture the righteous (Revelation 9:1–12).

Revelation describes them as follows:

> In appearance the locusts [Luther *Heuschrecken*] were like horses equipped for battle. On their heads were what looked like crowns of gold; their faces were like human faces, their hair like women's hair and their teeth like lions' teeth; they had scales like iron breastplates, and the noise of their wings was like the noise of many chariots with horses rushing into battle. They have tails like scorpions, with stingers, and in their tails is their power to harm people for five months. (9:7–10)

As with the lion-headed, serpent-tailed horses, here Cranach tries, somewhat in vain, to depict as much of this bizarre description of human-animal conglomeration as possible, creating an almost cartoonish creepiness. Their plump grasshopper bodies, covered in human armor, end in long thick tails with barbed stingers. They crawl and float over dead and dying people, their long blond hair flowing beneath their crowns, framing toothy grins on bearded faces.

FIGURE 6.4. Lucas Cranach the Elder, woodcut illustration of the fifth trumpet (Revelation 9:1–12) in Luther's September Testament, 1522. Image provided courtesy of the Richard C. Kessler Reformation Collection, Pitts Theology Library, Candler School of Theology, Emory University.

Emerging from the bottomless pit in the middle of the page is a huge, tree-shaped billow of flame and smoke. In its midst is the face of the angel surrounded by emanating rays of light. Partially curtained behind tongues of flame, he gazes sternly at the carnage below. While Cranach would likely have agreed with Rilke's famous line, "*jeder Engel ist schrecklich*" ("every angel is terrifying"), one cannot help but notice that this fire-engulfed angel is more terrifying than those drawn based on Dürer's illustrations. Rather than shy away from or naturalize John's monstrous apocalyptic imagination, Cranach offers an epiphany of divine monstrosity summoning forth horrific violence.

The Devil Wears Tiara

In other instances, Cranach taps into another of Revelation's monster-making potentials, namely, its usefulness in projecting ecclesiastical and political enemies as diabolically monstrous others. As David Price points out, the September Testament was the first print book designed with the "dual function of disseminating Scripture and inflaming popular opinion against the Catholic Church."[9] Much of the latter work was done via Cranach's illustrations. His depiction of fallen Babylon, "dwelling place of demons . . . haunt of every foul spirit," with whom all the kings of the earth have fornicated (Revelation 18:2–3), for example, is based on the Vatican and the nearby Castel Sant'Angelo (the mausoleum of Emperor Hadrian) in Rome. Still more provocative,

Cranach crowns both his whore of Babylon and his beast from the abyss in the temple (based on Revelation 11, with no parallel in Dürer) with papal tiaras, thereby associating these diabolical enemies of God with the Roman Catholic Church and its pope. After sharp criticism from George the Bearded, the Catholic Duke of Saxony, Cranach cut out the tiaras from the woodcut blocks so that they would not appear in subsequent printings.[10] The more subtle visual association of the Vatican with Babylon nonetheless remained. (Later, in Luther's complete Bible of 1534, Babylon is depicted as Worms, where the Edict of Worms outlawed Protestantism in the Holy Roman Empire.)

Cranach's association of the beast and the whore of Babylon with the pope in the September Testament found its way into the Geneva Bible, a very popular English translation produced in 1560 by English Puritan reformers who had fled to Switzerland to escape the persecutions of Protestants by Queen Mary (1516–58). A note in the first edition explicitly identifies the beast rising from the pit in Revelation 11 as the pope. Later editions went even further—the 1598 edition, for example, includes notes to Revelation that call Pope Gregory VII "a most monstrous Necromancer" and "a slave of the devil."[11]

We have already seen how, throughout its many lives, Revelation has frequently made itself useful as a kind of othering machine, as it does here and throughout the Reformation. Protestants use it to monstrocize Catholics, Catholics use it to monstrocize Protestants, and factions and individuals within each tradition use it to monstrocize other factions and individuals. After Cranach, these othering powers will increasingly be expressed in visual images. Indeed, this is not the last time we will see an apocalyptic beast wearing a tiara.

Luther Notwithstanding

Luther and Cranach's New Testament was a huge publishing success. Its first printing of between three and five thousand copies sold out almost immediately, and another large edition, the "December Testament," was printed two months later. There were at least eleven more reprints at other presses over the next year. In all, there were at least forty-three reprints, totaling at least 86,000 copies, published between 1522 and 1525.[12]

In 1534, Luther's translation of the entire Bible was published, including a new set of woodcuts by an otherwise unknown artist (initials "MS") from Cranach's workshop. It included copies of all twenty-one of Cranach's original illustrations of Revelation plus five new ones. While it also had eighty-two illustrations in the Old Testament, most of which were based on earlier illustrated Bibles, it had only seven non-Revelation illustrations in the New Testament (one for each Gospel, two of Paul, and one of Peter).

The success of Luther's whole Bible was as unprecedented as that of his New Testament. Its original publisher in Wittenberg, Hans Lufft, printed at least 100,000 copies over the next three decades, and numerous reprints and copies were published elsewhere in Germany. In some editions, the illustrations were printed from the original woodcut blocks, while others used smaller copies.

Soon nearly every German household had a copy of the Luther Bible, including the Cranach-based depictions of the visions from Revelation.[13] Whether they were reading the text of Revelation or not, they were very likely looking at its pictures. Indeed, in the early copies I have been able to examine, the high concentration of finger staining on the edges of the pages of Revelation alone is evidence of just such special attention from users (if not necessarily readers) of Luther's Bibles.[14]

Thus, in Luther's whole Bible as in his and Cranach's New Testament, Revelation is set apart visually from the rest of Scripture, not only by its heavy concentration of illustrations but also by the sheer supernatural strangeness of the images themselves—a strangeness that in many ways both mirrors and compounds the strangeness of the text. It lives in the back of the Bible as a kind of literary-visual apocalyptic tail, as weirdly out of place in the Bible as the snake tails are on Cranach's horses—and as disturbingly fascinating.

Not only were Cranach's Revelation woodcuts important to the success of Luther's Bibles, and therefore to this new life of Revelation in pictures. They enjoyed still more influence indirectly, through the many Bible illustrators that copied them in non-Luther Bibles. D. Johan Dietenberger's 1534 German translation, for example, which was meant as a Roman Catholic antidote to, or at least replacement of, Luther's Bible published the same year, includes twenty-one illustrations of Revelation, all very close to Cranach's, sans tiaras and Vatican imagery.[15] The lavishly detailed title page, with the pope enthroned front and center, announces Dietenberger's Bible as boldly Roman Catholic, making its debt to Cranach all the more striking.

Recall that what Luther hated most about the text of Revelation was that it dealt exclusively in uninterpreted "visions and images" that obscured more than they clarified. No doubt he especially disliked John's serpent-tailed horses and scorpion-tailed locusts, sent by God and his angels to wipe out or torture masses of humanity for no obvious reason. Luther would just as soon have seen Revelation fall out of the back of his Bible. But quite the opposite happened: many skipped to the end to see it. Thanks to Cranach's depictions of John's visions, which do little to help clarify or interpret their meaning but do much to highlight their weirdness, Luther's Bible gave Revelation a new, disturbingly supernatural vitality, popularizing it among hundreds of thousands of new readers.

New World of Gods and Monsters

Othering Other Religions

At the dawn of print culture and in the wake of Luther's Bible with Cranach's visual apocalypse, the expansion and proliferation of the multimedia constellation of Revelation accelerates. Attention to it as a literary whole diminishes as pieces of it—little story-shaped images, apocalyptic shards—detach from their literary biblical contexts and attach to new media ecologies, taking on new lives. In print media and beyond, what we have called the *generative incomprehensibility* of the images and mythemes of Revelation literally explodes.

The whore of Babylon, for example, will still often represent the Roman Catholic Church in many Protestant speculations, even to this day, as it did in Cranach's woodcut and in the notes of the extremely popular Geneva Bible (1560). But she will also stand for a feared one-world religious government, as in Hal Lindsey's *The Late, Great Planet Earth* (1970) and in the Jehovah's Witness *Watchtower Bible*. She will also give expression to masculine anxieties about powerful women. Just search the Internet for the phrase "whore of Babylon" along with the name

Hillary Clinton, Angela Merkel, or Michelle Obama, and you will find ample evidence of this othering trend. Likewise with the number 666, which often circulates quite independent from the context of John's vision as simply the encoded identity of a diabolical world leader, from United States President Ronald Wilson Reagan, with six characters per name (= 666), to Adolf Hitler, whose name adds up to 666 when one uses an alphanumeric key that counts from 100 (A = 100, B = 101, C = 102, etc.).

Hitler himself, on the other hand, identified his Nazi party with God's side of the battle in Revelation and his political opponents as those rejected by Christ. He heralded his envisioned Third Reich as the "Thousand Year Reich," equating it with the thousand-year reign of Christ inaugurated by the Second Coming (Revelation 20); and in his 1932 campaign, he accused his opponents of being lukewarm, like the Church in Laodicea (Revelation 3:15–16), so that God will spit them out. "In that [God] permits the destruction of the lukewarm," he declared, "He wishes thereby to give us victory."[1] Whether Hitler ever read the relevant scenes from Revelation, let alone the book of Revelation as a whole, is unknown, and does not matter. The images function effectively, indeed powerfully, within his rhetoric quite independent of their specific literary biblical context. Indeed, any detailed attention to them in context could diminish their power by questioning their applicability to the new context.[2]

As we proceed, then, we will find ourselves chasing these *generatively incomprehensible* fragments of Revelation into an ever-expanding multimedia field of apocalyptic imaginaries. Revelation survives and thrives by degrees of separation.

Chaos Gods

Remember that John did not conjure his monsters out of nowhere. Rather he stitched them together from the parts of past monsters dug up from Jewish prophetic texts and other ancient mythospheres. Chief among them is John's great red dragon, "that ancient serpent, who is the Devil and Satan" (Revelation 20:2). As previously noted, he bears striking family resemblances to Hebrew biblical chaos monsters, especially Leviathan and the "sea monster" (*tannin*) in Isaiah, Ezekiel, and Psalm 74, all of which get translated as *drakon*, "dragon," in the Greek Septuagint version of the Jewish Scriptures.

Look deeper down the gullet of John's dragon, moreover, and you may also notice even more ancient serpentine monsters and monster gods swimming around down there: the Hydra of Greek mythology, for example, who was slain by Hercules; or the Python, who threatened Leto's son Apollo; perhaps, too, the ancient Canaanite chaos gods Yamm and the seven-headed Litan (= Hebrew Leviathan); and perhaps, inside their bellies, the Babylonian chaos mother Tiamat, or the Vedic serpent-demon Vtra.[3]

So John made his monsters from other monsters. Once made, however, they took on lives of their own, migrating out of John's text altogether and into other imaginaries.

None has proven more slippery, more likely to migrate, than the diabolical dragon. We find him, for example, in the legend of Saint George, dating back to the sixth century, in which the hero (like the archangel Michael in Revelation 12) defeats the dragon, saves the princess, and thereby secures a promise from her father that all his subjects will be baptized. Here, then, the dragon is a threat to patriarchy, to the nation, and to eternal salvation.

We find this same diabolical dragon taking on new life in the Old English poem *Beowulf* as the abysmal, fire-breathing "earth-dragon" (*eorð-draca*) who terrorizes the Geat townspeople until he and the hero Beowulf finally slay one another. This dragon's ancientness, its identification with chaos and fiery destruction, and the fact that it is called both *draca* ("dragon") and *wyrm* ("worm" or "serpent") make clear its ancestry in Revelation. Like the diabolical dragon in the book of Revelation, and like Beowulf's earlier monstrous opponent, Grendel, this dragon is a chaos monster that threatens the divinely blessed social and cosmic order of creation.[4]

Here Be Dragons

There is another, more insidious tradition of monster-making that traces back to that great red dragon and other beasts of Revelation. It is the long history of translating the gods of unfamiliar, non-Western religious traditions into Western Christendom's devils—making monsters out of other people's gods.

Tales of Westerners confronted with monstrous forms while traveling in East and South Asia go back at least as far as the late thirteenth and fourteenth centuries, with the travel narratives of Marco Polo, Odoric de Pordenone, and Sir John Mandeville.[5] Their fantastical descriptions were later depicted in the illustrated early fifteenth-century *Livre des merveilles* and many other books that drew their visual vocabulary largely from Revelation. Marco Polo's huge, voracious dragons of the Carajan region in China, for example, which were depicted with huge wings and serpent heads at the ends of their tails, appear to be stitched together from the great winged dragon in Revelation 12 and the lion-faced horses with serpents for tails in Revelation 9.

It is likewise with scenes of purported encounters described by Odoric of Pordenone (1286–1331), a Franciscan monk and missionary who wrote a detailed account of his travels in Asia in the 1320s. Among the many marvels he describes is a corpse-strewn "perilous valley" in which dwells a winged devil who holds souls captive. What Odoric was actually facing, if anything, is uncertain, but may well have been a colossal statue of the Buddha. Yet, as art historian Partha Mitter points out, he and his illustrators were predisposed to find devil-monsters in Asia thanks to the "widely diffused fabulous tradition" of legends about the travels of Alexander the Great that described a great devil there, a devil that easily merged with John's great winged devil dragon.[6] Like those ancient maps on which *terra incognita*, unknown territory, was marked by the warning *hic sunt dracones*, "here be dragons," the Alexander legend plotted where one would find such a diabolical monster, and the Revelation tradition predicted what it would look like.

Devil of Calicut

Among the most popular monstrous projections of Revelation's devil onto Indian divinity was the "God of Calicut," first described by the Italian traveler and diarist Lodovico de Varthema in his *Itinerario* (1510) and then reprinted in subsequent editions and transposed into other travel narratives for centuries to follow. Indeed, for many Europeans, Varthema's God of Calicut came to epitomize India's theological imagination and its indigenous religious practices as diabolically monstrous.

While in the city of Calicut (Kozhikode) in southern India, Varthema's host, the "King of Calicut," whom he calls a "pagan who worships the devil," shows him a small chapel in his home. Here is Varthema's description of the chief's god as a kind of Satanic antipope surrounded by other devilish figures:

> His chapel is two paces wide in each of the four sides, and three paces high, with a wooden door covered with devils carved in relief. In the midst of this chapel there is a devil made of metal, placed in a seat also made of metal. The said devil has a crown made like that of the papal kingdom, with three crowns; and it also has four horns and four teeth, with a very large

mouth, nose, and most terrible eyes. The hands are made like those of a flesh-hook, and the feet like those of a cock; so that he is a fearful object to behold. All the pictures around the said chapel are those of devils, and on each side of it there is a Sathanas [i.e., Satan] seated in a seat, which seat is placed in a flame of fire, wherein are a great number of souls, of the length of half a finger and a finger of the hand. And the said Sathanas holds a soul in his mouth with the right hand, and with the other seizes a soul under the waist.[7]

A scene worthy of John of Patmos himself. As Mitter rightly observes, Varthema's language here draws heavily on medieval hell and Last Judgement imagery, which is largely drawn in turn from the apocalyptic imaginary of Revelation.[8] We might also note that this description of Satan as an amalgam of different creatures (horns and a crown, flesh hooks for hands, feet like a cock's) holding a soul in his mouth with his right hand and another in his other hand echoes not only Dante's description of the Devil in his *Inferno* but also, strangely, John's terrifying opening vision of the risen Christ, also a monstrous amalgamation of different elements, holding seven stars in his right hand and a sword in his mouth (Revelation 1:16), perhaps subconsciously attesting to the monstrosity of that divine image.

As with Odoric, it is impossible to know for sure what was actually there in the chapel of Varthema's host.[9] That is because what he describes is not so much Indian as it is

FIGURE 7.1. Jörg Breu, "The Idol of Calicut," woodcut illustration in the first German edition of Ludovico di Varthema, *Die Ritter-lich und lobwirdig rayss des gestrengen . . .* , 1516.

biblical. What he "saw" was his own projection of a devil monster of Revelation. It is likewise with Varthema's illustrators in subsequent editions of his *Itinerario*. The woodcut illustration by the Augsburg artist Jörg Breu the Elder in the 1516 German translation, for example, represents this scene as a kind of evil anti-Mass.[10]

Here the Satan that Varthema describes in the middle of the chapel merges with the monstrous figures on either side to become one. This horned devil, wearing a papal tiara, eats its meal of damned souls while a robed figure wafts incense with a censor. Thus, Breu's illustration combines familiar European visual images of Christian worship with apocalyptic images of hell and the Last Judgment—an unholy mix of religious familiarity and religious otherness.

Later travel narratives often appropriated Varthema's devil of Calicut even as they amplified the biblical apocalyptic sense of the scene. In his popular late sixteenth-century itinerary, for example, Jan Huygen van Linschoten (1563–1611), a Dutch merchant and explorer in the East Indies who served as secretary to the Portuguese Viceroy in Goa, India, expands the small chapel described by Varthema into what he calls a "Sancta Sanctorium, or rather Diabolorium" of a larger church, adding more horns and a second face to its devil-god, and making explicit the biblical connection with Revelation.

> At last wee came into a Village, where stoode a great Church of stone, wherein wee entered, and found nothing in it but a great [picture] that hung in the middle of the Church [with the Image of a Pagode painted therein] so mishaped and deformed, that more monsterous was never seene, for it had many horns, and long teeth that hung out of his mouth down to the knees, and beneath his Navel and belly it had an other such like face, with many hornes and tuskes. Uppon the head thereof stood a [triple-crowned] Myter, not much unlike the Popes triple crown, so that in effect it seemed to be a monster [such as are described] in the Apocalips.[11]

By the turn of the seventeenth century, then, we find a fairly standard European representation, in word and image, of Indian religion as worship of the apocalyptic devil-monsters of Revelation—casting adherents as masses hopelessly deceived by Satan and his beasts. This standard representation comes not from the rich diversity of India's religious visual cultures but from stock terms and conventional images taken from European traditions of biblical interpretation, especially from Revelation's written descriptions and illustrations of the devil-dragon and its beasts.[12]

These projections of familiar, at-hand apocalyptic imagery onto unfamiliar religious images and practices are common to colonial discourse. As Homi K. Bhabha observes, such projections produce the cultural other as "a social reality which is at once an 'other' and yet entirely knowable and visible."[13] The dynamic involves an ambivalent play of sameness and difference, attraction and repulsion, projecting one's own familiar images of monstrous evil onto an unfamiliar religious visual culture, reducing unique and irreducible difference to one's own system of meaning by making monsters of other peoples' gods. The translation of religious difference in a new world of apocalyptic monster gods does precisely that: it creates an image of familiar otherness that literally *orients* Western Christian identity against it.

A Little Demon Class

Tragically, many subsequent evangelistic movements of Christianity inherited this practice of projecting other people's gods as apocalyptic monsters whose aim is to deceive believers into worshiping them and their images. Lucy Evangeline Guinness, a Christian writer, editor, and missionary from London, and the cofounder of the Sudan United Mission, is exemplary of the ways this biblical vocabulary of apocalyptic beastly horror finds its way into calls to the mission field. Her book, *Across India at the Dawn of the 20th Century* (1898), which documents her travels with her father, the celebrated missionary Grattan Guinness, is rich with a millennial zeal for a mission to India. Lamenting a people she sincerely believes to be lost in devotion to demons and devils, she echoes John's vision of all of the earth's inhabitants worshiping the Devil as dragon, his two monstrous beasts, and the image of the beast (Revelation 13).

> O India! thy darkness is not the darkness of mere ignorance, but the darkness of lies, fantastic lies, foul lies, leprous lies, diabolical lies; thy shame is public.... Thy gods are grovelling, bestial.... They glower on their worshippers from filthy shrines; their name is legion, their legends [i]nfamous and monstrous; thy deities are demons, and thy Pantheon a Pandemonium, where millions made in the image of God prostrate themselves before beasts and devils as though they were divine.... Never hast thou known the light of revelation.... Who shall bring thee forth from thy dark prison-house, from thy horrid chambers of imagery?[14]

Appealing to Western Christians to support missionary efforts in India, Guinness grieves these "millions made in the image of God" as victims, deceived by false gods that she believes, in "the light of revelation," will be exposed as a "Pandemonium" of "beasts and devils."[15]

CHAPTER 7

Over the last century, we have witnessed such evangelistic monster-making of other peoples' religions take root "back home" in the Christian West. In many respects, the rise of the Christian Right since the 1960s, in the United States and elsewhere, can be understood as a backlash against growing religious diversity.[16] Although the most obvious platforms on which that movement has established itself have been antiabortion and antihomosexuality, its loudest proponents have from the beginning also frequently decried non-Christian religions, especially Buddhism and Hinduism, as monstrously other forms of devil worship.

Television evangelist, Christian Coalition leader, and 1988 presidential candidate Pat Robertson, for example, has long believed that Christians who practice yoga are inadvertently worshiping the Devil: They "are actually not in touch with some great 'God consciousness' or psychic power but Satan and demons."[17] This he ties to apocalyptic expectations, based primarily on his understanding of Revelation, that a "new world order" will soon be established in which Christians will no longer be free to resist Satan and his beasts disguised as gods.[18]

This belief that yoga is a gateway to worshiping Satan or his beast is common in conservative Christian circles to this day. Celebrity pastor Mark Driscoll, formerly of Mars Hill Church in Seattle, Washington, has often decried the spiritual dangers of yoga. In a 2010 sermon, for example, he declared that Christians must stay away from yoga: "Yoga is demonic. If you just sign up for a little yoga class, you're signing up for a little demon class."[19]

Often such warnings are linked to the idea that, by participating in another religion's meditative practices, one unwittingly becomes possessed by the "kingdom of darkness." "Doing these Eastern spiritual practices is aligning yourself with the kingdom of darkness," one recent self-proclaimed witch-turned-Christian explained in a 2016 online video testimonial. "Once you bring these practices into your life, you are also inviting these demonic entities into your home and your family."[20] Similarly, in a 2015 Catholic Mass in Drumsurn, Ireland, Father Roland Colhoun warned that "both practicing yoga and getting Indian head massages will lead to the Kingdom of Darkness."[21]

This idea of the "kingdom of darkness" is drawn from the New Testament letter to the Colossians, in which Paul writes that God "has rescued us from the power [*exousias*, "control" or "dominion'] of darkness and transferred us into the kingdom of his beloved Son." There, it is an entirely positive image of enlightenment, that is, of being brought out of the ignorance of darkness and into the light of the reign of God. In Augustine's *The City of God*, however, this "power of darkness" becomes synonymous with the domain of that other, worldly city (i.e., not the city of God), which is hopelessly lost to the devil and ultimately doomed to eternal damnation in the Last Judgment after the "second resurrection" described in Revelation.[22]

For Augustine, who believed some were predestined to the city of God and others to eternal damnation, the "kingdom of darkness" has no power over the faithful. More often, however, Christian theologians have seen this kingdom as an ever-present peril, a place into which one can easily be seduced by demonic powers at work in the world.[23] This belief, combined with the prevalent Christian strategy of projecting the deities of other religions as apocalyptic devils, is what drives the intense fear among many Christians that something so seemingly harmless, indeed peaceful, as yoga or Buddhist meditation could pave the way to hell. Salvation, they believe, is not predestined; it can be lost simply by not keeping guard against evil powers all around. There is a slippery slope, they warn, from salvation to the kingdom of darkness, and the devils of yoga and other forms of non-Christian meditation are always looking for weaknesses in one's faith.

Deliverance

In many respects, the gods-turned-monsters within the apocalyptic imaginaries of kingdom-of-darkness-wary Christians have come a long way from Varthema's devil of Calicut to Driscoll's "little demon class" of Seattle. In other respects, they are very close. Let me conclude with a story that brings together the apocalyptic fear of yoga as the devil's highway to the kingdom of darkness with the early colonialist projections of Indian deities as apocalyptic devil-dragons and beasts with which we began this chapter.

Corinna had been a yoga practitioner and instructor for ten years.[24] She knew that many Christians think yoga is demonic, but she disagreed. Feeling strong in her Christian faith, she recalls, "I balked at the idea that the devil could have any intellectual property right in certain body positions or movements."

Then, after a pastor (on whose website she tells her story) cast out "a demon of oriental medicine" from her, she began to worry about her yoga as well. "Having been broadsided by the discovery that I had a demon of oriental medicine, I became open to the possibility that I might have a demon of yoga as well." What if the Holy Spirit were being replaced by "a Hindu spirit," she worried, inadvertently conjured by her yoga practice?

She fasted and prayed, pleading to God for an answer. Then, as she puts it, "He kindly gave me a nightmare." Here is her description:

> I found myself in a gym setting like the ones where I taught yoga. A woman was reclining on a yoga mat. She said to me, "I live here." Next to her, a gargantuan bodybuilder was doing a military press. Then I found myself in my home office, where I had prepared class materials like yoga syllabi, choreography, and handouts. I lit something like incense or pot, and the smoke arose. Then I looked out the window into my backyard and gasped. There was a huge, inflatable, phosphorescent altar to Hindu deities and a banqueting table with a place set for me. I was gripped with fear and wanted it cleared from my property, but a giant festive dragon flew like a kite or windsock up to the window and rattled its face at me. I cursed it and pounded on the window, but it wouldn't retreat until I yelled for Jesus.

She began reflecting on the nightmare. Why were the figures of Indian deities and the dragon toy-like? Because, she decided, she had been toying around with something dangerous, unawares.

Now convinced that she did indeed have a yoga demon, she stood in front of a mirror so that she could see it as it was exorcised. When she commanded it to leave, she recalls, it initially manifested itself as a pleasant "surge of energy—a full body rush to my head." But that did not last.

> Then a fierce, ugly, snake-like expression settled on my face. The upsurge of energy and the snake face were in line with Hindu paintings of kundalini energy coiled like a cobra at the base of the spine and rising to the third eye or crown of the head of the aspiring yogi.

At first, the demon claimed to serve Christ, but under pressure it confessed that it served Satan. She "cross examined it by the power of the Holy Spirit" and learned that it possessed innocent people by lying to them about the harmlessness of yoga as a simple exercise practice. "By this deceit," she writes, "it lures unwitting Christians into idolatry with promises of weight loss, physical fitness and stress reduction."

Such testimonials concerning the diabolical otherness of yoga are, of course, different from the horrid chambers of imagery conjured in century-old missionary accounts, not to mention Varthema in Calicut. Yet they all take part in a shared genealogy of monstrocizing religious otherness that traces itself back to Revelation, the monster-maker's Bible. As I have said before, Revelation is an othering machine. With it between me and the world, difference, especially religious difference, translates into diabolical otherness—anti-me, anti-us, anti-God.

You are weak, we are told, but they are strong. These other gods, these devils, they will beguile you, seduce you, draw you into the kingdom of darkness. It starts with a little seemingly harmless yoga, or Buddhist meditation, or Chinese medicine. Next thing you know, you are eating food sacrificed to idols (Revelation 2:14, 20). You are learning unawares "the deep things of Satan" (2:24). You are worshiping the dragon who is Satan, its beasts, and the image of the beast (13:1–15)—and you have taken its mark (13:16–18).

·In the process, such apocalyptic monster-making has the potential to deny the actual vulnerability of the one being monstrocized—the visitor, the immigrant, the foreigner, the marginal. Denying their humanity can help justify violence against them. Indeed, it not only can help justify violence, it can ordain and bless it as part of a cosmic battle of good versus evil, God versus Satan, which will culminate in a final judgment, for which we had better be ready.

Heaven in a Garage

James Hampton's Throne Room

After this I looked, and, behold, a door was opened in heaven: and the first voice which I heard was as it were of a trumpet talking with me; which said, Come up hither, and I will shew thee things which must be hereafter. And immediately I was in the spirit: and, behold, a throne was set in heaven, and one sat on the throne. And he that sat was to look upon like a jasper and a sardine stone: and there was a rainbow round about the throne, in sight like unto an emerald. And round about the throne were four and twenty seats: and upon the seats I saw four and twenty elders sitting, clothed in white raiment; and they had on their heads crowns of gold. (Revelation 4:1–4; King James Version)

He was "working on something" that no longer fit in his boardinghouse room, he had told the landlord when he began renting the old brick garage on Seventh Street Northwest in Washington, DC, in 1950 for $50 a month. And for fourteen years this quiet, unassuming African-American man who sometimes called himself St. James never missed a payment—until now. It was December 1964, the rent was well past due, and the landlord had heard nothing from him.

In fact, James Hampton had died of stomach cancer the month before, leaving no instructions for anyone about what to do with whatever he had been working on in the garage.

Intending to clear out the space and find a new renter, the landlord broke the padlock, rolled open the heavy wooden door, and turned on the lights. To his astonishment, he found himself standing before a dazzling array of silver, gold, and purple winged thrones, glimmering altarpieces, bedazzled crowns, and other lustrous objects, all flooded with the light of a dozen 500-watt bulbs hanging from the rafters overhead. And at the center of everything stood a seven-foot-high, brilliantly ornate throne, with silver wings spread wide over this garaged sanctuary like some back-alley seraphim. Above the throne were written the famous first words spoken by every biblical angel: "FEAR NOT."

The landlord was awestruck, but he also had business to take care of. After contacting Hampton's surviving sister, who wanted nothing to do with the garage or its contents, he put an ad in the paper in order to find another renter. It so happened that a sculptor answered the ad. Overwhelmed by the sight of Hampton's throne room, he called Alice Denney, a major art collector in the Washington, DC area. Likewise amazed, she invited several more artists, curators, and congressmen to come and see. While Denney was trying to acquire the work from Hampton's

FIGURE 8.1. James Hampton, *The Throne of the Third Heaven of the Nations' Millennium General Assembly*, c. 1950–64, mixed media. Smithsonian American Art Museum. Gift of anonymous donors.

sister, another curator, Harry Lowe, laid claim to it for the Smithsonian simply by paying the landlord the back rent.

Considered by many to be the greatest work of American folk art, James Hampton's material vision of the divine throne room of Revelation, known as *The Throne of the Third Heaven of the Nations' Millennium General Assembly*, is now a permanent installation in the Smithsonian American Art Museum.

Life Work

In the years since the discovery and acquisition of Hampton's *Throne*, research has uncovered only fragments of his life story.[1] Born in 1909 in the small rural town of Elloree, South Carolina, he moved to Washington, DC, in 1928, at the age of nineteen. Hampton worked as a short-order cook among other odd jobs until, in 1942, he was drafted into the United States Army to serve as part of a segregated unit in which he did carpentry and maintained airstrips in Saipan and Guam during World War II. After being honorably discharged in 1945, he returned to the DC area and took a job as a night janitor for the General Administration Services, where he worked until his death in 1964.

Much of his biography comes from inscriptions in the throne room itself. One inscription on a small, shrine-like object (now situated front and center of the museum exhibit) reads, "Made on Guam, April 14, 1945," indicating that he must have already been working on it during his time in the army.

Inscriptions on other works testify that he began having visions much earlier, within a few years of his move to DC. One reads, "This is true, that the great Moses, the giver of the 10th commandment, appeared in Washington April 11, 1931." Another reads, "This is true that on October 2, 1946, the great Virgin Mary and the Star of Bethlehem appeared over the nation's capital." And another reads, "This is true that Adam, the first man God created, appeared in person on January 20, 1949. This was on the day of President Truman's inauguration."

"That's my life," Hampton had once told his landlord, "I'll finish it before I die."[2] Indeed, such works in progress tend to last exactly as long as their creators' lives do. Whether recreating the Holy Land in Virginia, Noah's Ark in Maryland, or heaven's throne room in Washington, DC, the creator and the creation are coterminous. The creation literally becomes the life of its creator and ends when his or her life ends.

Revelation Becomes Him

Hampton's *Throne* is an overwhelming vision of mysterious otherness emerging from seeming familiarity, a revelation of the sacred in the profane. There are 180 objects in all, most bearing only the faintest traces of their former, domestic lives as everyday household things: used chairs and tables, for example, that have been cut in half or otherwise altered, built up, and augmented into winged heavenly bodies by adding cardboard tubing, insulation board, dead light bulbs, ink blotters, and other discards, and then heavily adorned with silver aluminum foil and gold foil from liquor bottle labels and candy bar wrappers.

Hampton's throne room is indeed a work of creative genius, well deserving of its prominent place in the Smithsonian collection as a centerpiece of American art. Still, what if religionists and biblical scholars rather than artists and curators had been the first to discover it? In the context of the exhibit in the Smithsonian, the scriptural dimensions of this remarkable life work as a material, spatial enactment of Revelation can be over-looked or at least diminished in the process of appreci-ating it as artistic expression.

Also found in the garage were black-and-white photo-graphs of Hampton with his work. In one, he wears a dark suit and a handmade crown while holding another crown in his hands. There are seven of these crowns, each made of gold-foil-covered cardboard with a silver-foil-covered light bulb on the top. On the front of each crown is a gold plate with typescript reading,

THE NATIONS
MILLENNIUM GENERAL
ASSEMBLY
Revelation 7, Verse 3

The biblical reference is to the scene in which an angel descends from the sun and seals 144,000 servants of God, 12,000 from each of the twelve tribes of Israel (Rev-elation 7:3–8). This scene is immediately followed by

FIGURE 8.2. James Hampton, *Crown from The Throne of the Third Heaven of the Nations' Millennium General Assembly*, c. 1950–64, gold and silver aluminum foil, cardboard, found objects. Smithsonian American Art Museum. Gift of Margaret Kelley McHugh, Nancy Kelley Schneider, and William H. Kelley.

what Hampton must be envisioning as the glorious "nations' general assembly" to come:

> After this I looked, and there was a great multitude that no one could count, from every nation, from all tribes and peoples and languages, standing before the throne and before the Lamb, robed in white, with palm branches in their hands.... And all the angels stood around the throne and around the elders and the four living creatures, and they fell on their faces before the throne and worshiped God. (Revelation 7:9, 11)

FIGURE 8.3. Unidentified photographer, James Hampton with *The Throne of the Third Heaven of the Nations' Millennium General Assembly*. Courtesy of the Smithsonian American Art Museum.

In the photo, then, a crowned Hampton is ordaining himself among those righteous ones assembled from all the nations before God.

Another photo depicts Hampton, holding an ornately decorated book or plaque, standing in front of the entire throne room space.

In the lower left corner of the photo, he has attached a small piece of paper with a handwritten caption that reads,

THE THiRD HEAVEN

THE SECOND-CORiNTHiAST

12 - 2 - 3

Hampton is associating his sanctuary with the "third heaven" mentioned in Paul's second letter to the Corinthians in the New Testament. There Paul says he knows a man who, fourteen years earlier, was "caught up to the third heaven . . . caught up into Paradise and heard inexpressible words" (2 Corinthians 12:2–4). Many believe Paul was actually referring to himself. In any case, with this reference as a caption for his photo, Hampton lays claim to that biblical revelation for himself: not only is his throne room an incarnation of that biblical "third heaven" in which Paul or someone Paul knew "heard inexpressible words"; Hampton has been there himself and received such revelations.

In fact, Hampton also wrote a 108-page book entitled *St. James: The Book of the 7 Dispensation*, which is something of a recording of his own "inexpressible words." Apart from its title and the words "St. James" and "Revelation" at the top and bottom of each page, the entire notebook is written in Hampton's own yet-to-be-deciphered script—a doubly encoded revelation.

With his throne room sanctuary, Hampton links Paul's passing reference to a "third heaven" of mystical experience to John's vision of the sparkling, heavenly throne room and to the assembly of the 144,000. This throne and its glorious surroundings are then linked to yet another idea developed from the book of Revelation, namely the Second Coming and enthronement of Christ and the resurrection of the saints who will reign with him for a millennium, or one thousand years:

FIGURE 8.4. James Hampton, *The Book of the 7 Dispensation*, c. 1945–64, commercially printed ledger, cardboard, ink, and foil. Smithsonian American Art Museum. Gift of Harry Lowe.

Then I saw thrones, and those seated on them were given authority to judge. I also saw the souls of those who had been beheaded for their testimony to Jesus and for the word of God. They had not worshiped the beast or its image and had not received its mark on their foreheads or their hands. They came to life and reigned with Christ a thousand years. (Revelation 20:4)

Thus, in Hampton's throne room, the bedazzling enthronement scene in Revelation 4 becomes the very scene of the Second Coming and the thousand-year reign of Christ envisioned in Revelation 20. Likewise, the twenty-four elders seated around the central throne in the earlier vision become the saints who will be resurrected from the dead and reign with Christ in the new millennium in the later vision.

Hampton's fuller naming of his work, *The Throne of the Third Heaven of the Nations' Millennium General Assembly*, which appears on several of the objects, links these two visions of divine enthronement with the final, climactic vision of a new heaven, a new earth, and a new Jerusalem at the end of the book of Revelation. There, after the former heaven and earth pass away, the shining holy city descends to earth and all the nations gather there to "walk by its light, and the kings of the earth will bring their glory into it," and the city's gates "will never be shut by day—and there will be no night there" (Revelation 21:24–25).

In Hampton's vision, then, multiple images of enthronement and assembly from Revelation fold onto one another across time on the shimmering staging space of his garage: John's early visions of the throne room in heaven (Revelation 4) and the assembly of the 144,000 saints (Revelation 7) become not only the scene of the Second Coming and millennial reign of Christ on his throne (Revelation 20) but also the scene of the coming of the New Jerusalem and what Hampton calls "the nations' millennium general assembly" after the Last Judgment (Revelation 21).

Hampton built his throne room not only to imagine and anticipate the coming of the new millennium and the reign of God on earth; he built it to *host* that coming. It is a space of creative apocalyptic hospitality.

Staging Revelation

The individual objects of Hampton's throne room testify to and deepen this multilayered biblical conception of the space, even as they push further beyond any straightforward biblical interpretation or reception.

Nearly all of the 180 pieces bear handwritten biblical messages on small paper labels, some written in English capitals and some written in Hampton's own undeciphered script. Of those in English, some are biblical quotations, some are Hampton's own comments and biblical glosses, and some are biblical references (many from the book of Revelation). Most of the biblical quotations appear to have been written from memory, as they often include unusual spellings and do not appear to come from any particular biblical translation.

Every object in Hampton's throne room is quite literally a biblical object, a thing with biblical words, references, and comments inscribed all over it. So, too, the collection as a whole, which is a material staging of the Bible that is given structure and plot through references to and quotations from the book of Revelation.

Much like Joachim's visual mappings of biblical history via Revelation, the space of Hampton's throne room is built according to a highly complex system of symmetrical relationships between things and texts, all organized around the central throne, awaiting Christ's reign on earth. This symmetry operates on several levels.

First, each individual object is built according to a bilateral symmetry, so that if it were divided vertically each half would mirror the other.

Second, with the exception of the throne in the center of the room, each object on one side of the space pairs with an identical one on the other side.

Third, the symmetrical space of the room divides the Christian Bible between Old and New Testaments in a series of correspondences. To the right of the central throne (stage right, house left), all of the biblical texts are either quotations from or references to the text of the New Testament, mostly Revelation. To the far right, on the wall, like stained glass windows in a sanctuary, there are plaques with the names of the twelve apostles of Christ. To the left of the central throne (stage left, house right), all the biblical texts are either quotations from or references to the Old Testament, and to their left on the wall are plaques with names of Old Testament prophets. In this way the space presents a symmetrical interpretation of the Christian Bible in which details from Old Testament history are made to correspond to details from New Testament history, all of which culminate in Revelation.

On the back of one of the smaller thrones to the left, for example, there is a hand-drawn image of the two tablets of the Ten Commandments that Moses received on Mount Sinai. The words of the commandments themselves are not written out but are represented simply by columns of roman numerals: I–V on the first tablet, and VI–X on the second. To either side of the tablets are glyphs, presumably part of Hampton's own language script. Above the tablets is written, "I AM THAT I AM." And below the tables are the following lines:

AND GOD SPEAK ALL
THESE WORDS SAYING
I AM THE LORD THY GOD
WHIH HAVE BROUGHT
THE OUT OF THE LAND OF

Below these lines, standing alone in large capital letters, is the name "MOSES."

While this constellation of words around images of the tablets may seem random, it is not. All the elements are related to God's deliverance of the Hebrew people from slavery in Egypt and the subsequent giving of the law. The statement at the top, "I am that I am," is God's mysterious self-naming from the burning bush when Moses asks who he should say sent him to deliver his people (Exodus 3:14). Hampton's next lines, from "and God spoke" to "out of the land of," come immediately before God delivers the Ten Commandments themselves to Moses on Mount Sinai, after the exodus (Exodus 20:1–2). From here forward in the biblical narrative of the Torah, this will be the primary means by which God self-describes as the God of deliverance from Egypt. Thus, Hampton's image links the giving of the law to deliverance from slavery and places the relationship between God and Moses at the core of this Old Testament era of biblical history.

One effect of this intricate symmetry, as the late evolutionary biologist and historian of science Stephen Jay Gould noted in an essay on Hampton's throne room, is to integrate two different Christian biblical conceptions of time.[3] On the one hand, there is linear time, "time's arrow," as Gould puts it. Time's arrow sees history moving in a singular direction, from divine promise to fulfillment, from creation to new creation, from Genesis to Revelation. On the other hand, there is circular time, "time's cycle," which sees history repeating itself, with events of the past mirroring or foreshadowing events of the present and future.

Hampton's throne room is both arrow and cycle, encompassing both linear and circular time. On the one hand, its movement from an Old Testament era of history on the one side of the room to a New Testament era on the other suggests the familiar Christian linear understanding of biblical history, from "Law" to "Gospel" and from creation to redemption. On the other hand, the intricate symmetry of the two sides matches and links events from the Old Testament to those of the New Testament as mirrorings or correlations of one another. These correlations suggest that biblical history is a series of overlays, with the central throne of the Second Coming and millennial reign as the unifying center and consummation of all time.

For Hampton, moreover, the interpretive key to decoding both conceptions of biblical time is the book of Revelation, whose visions are integrated throughout the space. Here, as with Joachim, Revelation is both the culmination of the history of creation and the key to understanding all former biblical eras in relation to this final culmination.

Dispensations

As the title of his notebook, *The Book of the 7 Dispensation*, suggests, a central feature of Hampton's apocalyptic faith as expressed in his throne room is the Christian theology of dispensationalism. With roots going back to Joachim's illustrated theories of the interrelated eras of biblical history, dispensationalism became popular in the 1800s and early 1900s thanks especially to the works of John Nelson Darby (1800–1882), Clarence Larkin (1850–1924), mentioned earlier as an apocalyptic heir of Joachim, and Cyrus I. Scofield (1843–1921), best known for the *Scofield Reference Bible*, a touchstone of biblical fundamentalism. Very like Joachim, these theologians envisioned the history of creation—past, present, and future—as a series of interrelated eras, each governed by a new "dispensation" of divine grace accompanied by a new covenantal agreement with humankind. Each dispensation, then, begins with a new revelation of God and ends with God's judgment of humankind's behavior according to that new revelation.

The most common school of dispensationalism, illustrated in Larkin's popular visual diagrams, has seven dispensations, all leading to a final dispensation that will have no end:

(1) the Edenic Dispensation (from creation through the fall of Adam and Eve and their expulsion from paradise);

(2) the Antedeluvian Dispensation (from the fall through the flood);

(3) the Postdeluvian Dispensation (from the new covenant with Noah through the scattering of humankind at the tower of Babel);

(4) the Patriarchal Dispensation (from the promise to Abraham through the forty-year wandering in the wilderness);

(5) the Legal Dispensation (from Israel under the Torah in the promised land through the crucifixion of Jesus Christ);

(6) the Ecclesiastical Dispensation (from Christ's resurrection through the history of the Christian church); and

(7) the Millennial Dispensation (the thousand-year reign of Christ with the saints, beginning with his Second Coming and concluding with the consummation of creation).

This seventh dispensation will be followed by the consummation of all things, beginning with the Last Judgment and the creation of the new heaven, new earth, and new Jerusalem as described in Revelation.

Note that this scenario differs from Augustine's in *The City of God*. There, the millennial reign of Christ with the saints is already well underway, having begun with the resurrection and the establishment of Christ's church. Here, as in apocalyptic scenarios prior to Augustine's, the Second Coming, which has yet to come, will inaugurate that millennial dispensation.

Hampton's throne room attests to his belief that human history was nearing the end of the sixth dispensation, that is, the Ecclesiastical Dispensation, and awaiting the seventh dispensation, which would be inaugurated by the Second Coming and enthronement of Christ. Thus would commence Christ's reign alongside the resurrected saints in what Hampton called "the nations' millennium general assembly."

At the same time, for Hampton as for Joachim nearly a millennium before, all these biblical texts are linked together and integrated in a larger, totalizing system via concordances with the book of Revelation, which once again serves as the codec, encoding and decoding all of biblical history, from creation to consummation.

Indeed, while worlds apart in so many ways, Hampton and Joachim are kindred prophetic spirits. Much as Joachim's figures brought word into image to encompass the entire history of creation, decoding what was encoded in Revelation, so Hampton's throne room integrates word into image, object, and space to create an architecture that both explicates history and sets the stage for its glorious culmination.

Yet Hampton's work is also something even more radically new. Whereas Joachim mapped his vision of biblical time in words and images on the flat surface of the page, Hampton built his into a three-dimensional space of staged objects. Thus Hampton's life work takes Revelation beyond description but also beyond depiction, into a lived space in which past, present, and future fold into one another.

Hampton himself occupied that space. He lived into it while working out its elaborate biblical apocalyptic imaginary. Indeed, attending now to its material details, one cannot help but imagine him working through the night to carefully transform the most mundane, everyday things into a revelation of Revelation. It must have been for him less about the final product than it was about the ongoing process. It was a religious practice, a means for him to meditate on, think through, long for, and ultimately host Christ, his kingdom come, and a new heaven and earth.

Left Behind, Again

The Rise and Fall of Evangelical Rapture Horror Culture

Growing up conservative evangelical in the late 1970s and early 1980s in Anchorage, Alaska, one of my favorite church youth group songs was called "I Wish We'd All Been Ready."[1] Originally written and performed in 1969 by Christian rock patriarch Larry Norman, the song paints a vivid scenario of a world after the rapture, a world absent not only of God but also of all true believers. "Life was filled with guns and war," the song begins, "and everyone got trampled on the floor. I wish we'd all been ready." Children are dying, the sun grows dark and cold. Food is so scarce that "a piece of bread could buy a bag of gold." A grim scene. But what was most horrifying about this doomsday scenario was that it was a world after God. "There's no time to change your mind," the chorus laments, "The Son has come, and you've been left behind."

We must have sung that song more than a hundred times during youth fellowship meetings. No one made eye contact. We all looked at the floor, feeling the weight of the words, as if we were the ones Christ had left behind when he returned to rapture his followers up to heaven. The song invited us to imagine a time when it was already too late, when our ambivalence, our lack of faith, had left us each alone, without God and, perhaps more terrifying at that age, without friends.

I had no idea that Larry Norman was the song's original writer and performer. I had never heard of him. I assumed the original version was the one sung by the Des Moines, Iowa group called the Fishmarket Combo during the opening credits of the 1972/3 evangelical rapture horror movie, *A Thief in the Night*, which we watched every year or so.[2] Then again, like most youth group kids in America, I was pretty much oblivious to everything going on in the larger world of Christian youth culture at the time.

The Rise of Evangelical Pop Culture

The late 1960s and early 1970s were big years for American evangelicalism generally and evangelical youth culture specifically. Emerging since the 1940s out of and in some ways against the fundamentalist movement, which had become increasingly countercultural and sectarian in the wake of the Scopes Trial and other embarrassments, "neo-evangelicalism," as it was then called, made American youth culture its mission field.[3] It sought to make its gospel popular by the world's standards. In the perennial Protestant Christian dilemma of preservation versus popularization—protecting and preserving the sanctity of the tradition versus getting the Word out by whatever means necessary—evangelicals leaned hard toward popularization, taking as their motto Paul's declaration, "I have become all things to all people, so that I might by any means save some" (1 Corinthians 9:22).

Central to their approach were para–church organizations such as Youth for Christ, Campus Crusade for Christ, and Young Life, which explicitly targeted the most popular kids with the expectation that others would follow. Their weekly club meetings included wild and crazy games and skits along with more serious (if brief) Bible study and prayer. Youth for Christ had actually begun as a series of Saturday-night youth rallies that attracted hundreds of thousands of young people in big cities across the United States. These rallies were led by young, energetic preachers like Billy Graham (the first full-time employee of Youth for Christ) and were modeled on the big shows popular in the emerging secular entertainment industry. Organizers produced slick ads and created mainstream radio and television tie-ins. Some of the evangelists went so far as to adopt the voices and styles of celebrities like Frank Sinatra. Others, like Graham, soon found their own distinctive star power.

By the early 1970s, neo-evangelical rallies were looking less like a Frank Sinatra show and more like a Led Zeppelin concert. In 1972, Campus Crusade for Christ hosted Explo '72, a weeklong gathering of high school and college students in Dallas, Texas. The event culminated in what was later dubbed the Christian Woodstock, an eight-hour-long Christian rock concert in the

Cotton Bowl that drew over 100,000 people and featured none other than Larry Norman and his mega hit rapture song, "I Wish We'd All Been Ready."

Rapture Theory

As an evangelical youth group kid, I assumed that the expectation voiced in Norman's song—that believers will be raptured into heaven and unbelievers will be left behind as all hell breaks loose on earth—was a cornerstone of Christianity and had been since Jesus. In fact, rapture theory is a rather recent development in the history of Christian thought. It originated in the early nineteenth century with the work of the dispensationalist theologian John Nelson Darby, mentioned in the previous chapter. Since then it has gained tremendous popularity among end-times–oriented Christians, thanks especially to its incorporation into the notes and illustrations of study Bibles like the *Scofield Reference Bible* (1909), the flagship study Bible of the early fundamentalist movement, and thanks to its centrality in popular end-times books like Hal Lindsey's 1970 bestseller, *The Late, Great Planet Earth*.[4]

Although most presume that the biblical book of Revelation is the blueprint for rapture theory, that text describes no such event.[5] Rather, rapture theory is another apocalyptic monster, stitched together from a few biblical fragments gathered from disparate sources. Three texts in particular:

- The promise in Revelation's letter to the church in Philadelphia that "because you have kept my word of patient endurance, I will keep you from the hour of trial that is coming on the whole world to test the inhabitants of the earth" (Revelation 3:10);
- the assurance in Paul's letter to the Thessalonians that, after God raises from the dead those believers who have already passed, "Then we who are alive, who are left, will be caught up in the clouds together with them to meet the Lord in the air; and so we will be with the Lord forever" (1 Thessalonians 3:17); and
- Paul's declaration to the church at Corinth that "we will all be changed, in a moment, in the twinkling of an eye, at the last trumpet. For the trumpet will sound, and the dead will be raised imperishable, and we will be changed." (1 Corinthians 15:51–52)

Building from these fragments an image of the saved, dead and alive, being raptured up from the earth to heaven, this rapture theory is then inserted back into Revelation as an event that, although not explicitly described in the text, will take place before the reign of Satan and his beasts. During that time of terror, those "left behind" will be forced to worship the beast and take its mark, or be persecuted and killed.

In many respects, evangelicalism was a far cry from the fundamentalism out of which it was born. Whereas fundamentalism was more sectarian, intentionally setting itself apart from mainstream society and popular culture, evangelicalism was, and is, all about making Christianity popular, adopting cultural trends and new media technologies in order to appeal to as many people as possible.

Yet, however different it looks in practice, evangelical theology essentially adopted fundamentalist theology wholesale. That meant not only carrying forward the fundamentalist view of the Bible as the literal, infallible Word of God; it also meant carrying forward other fundamentalist theories that were less obviously biblical, most notably the theory of the pretribulation rapture of the saints.

Cinematic Raptures

Emerging alongside other forms of neo-evangelical entertainment in the 1940s was a robust Christian film industry, which produced, promoted, and distributed evangelical feature films in the familiar styles of Hollywood and B movies to show in local churches, libraries, school gyms, and community theaters.[6]

One of the more successful of these companies in the early years was Charles O. Baptista's Scriptures Visualized Institute. Not only did Baptista's company produce dozens of evangelistic films for wide distribution; it also sold its own movie projector, called the Miracle Projector, which had a label guaranteeing that it would be "good until the second coming of Christ."[7]

In 1941, Baptista produced the very first evangelical rapture movie, called *The Rapture*. In documentary war-reel style, and no doubt haunted by the thousands of soldiers disappearing every day, this twelve-minute, sixteen-millimeter film includes many shots, cuts, and special effects that would become standard fare for rapture movies to follow: trains without conductors and other unmanned vehicles crashing into each other, empty cradles, and people disappearing while perplexed others are left behind, all interspersed with an antiphonal text message in the sky, asking, "Are you ready?" *The Rapture* was a big hit, shown in churches and at youth rallies across the United States for many years.

But no rapture movie has been more widely watched and more influential on American culture or on the emergence of evangelical horror culture than the 1972/3 movie, *A Thief in the Night*, the story of a young newly-wed, Patty, who awakes one morning to find the rapture has happened, taking her recently converted husband and leaving her behind in a world now abandoned by God and dominated by the powers of evil, represented by a one-world government called UNITE, which stands for "United Nations Imperium of Total Emergency."

The film is structured as a kind of rapture nightmare loop. It begins with an alarm clock waking Patty to radio reports of the sudden disappearance of millions of people around the world and the establishment of UNITE to maintain peace and order. Realizing that her husband, who had recently become a Christian, is among the missing, she collapses back onto her bed. At this point, the

FIGURE 9.1. Theatrical release poster for *A Thief in the Night*, 1973.

film cuts to a long series of recollections of events leading up to this moment, including sermons, a performance by the Fishmarket Combo, and conversations with her husband and others who had converted. Then, after a brief scene of the rapture, which depicts the lead singer of the Fishmarket Combo suddenly disappearing while mowing his lawn, the story cuts back to the post-rapture world, in which UNITE is imprisoning anyone who refuses to take its mark—a stamp image of three columns of zeros and ones digitally representing the number 666. After a long chase scene, Patty is cornered on a bridge. Instead of surrendering, she jumps, presumably to her death. She then wakes up, again, to her alarm and the radio reports, realizing that it was all a dream—but also, now, a reality.

The film's production company, Mark IV Pictures (a reference to Mark 4:33, "With many such parables he spoke the word to them, as they were able to hear it"), was a collaboration of Russell S. Doughten Jr., a longtime Christian, and Donald W. Thompson, a new and zealous convert to the faith. Both had extensive experience producing and directing secular films, including B-movie horror and action features. Their ambition was to make Christian action-adventure movies for young people.

Thief was shot entirely in Des Moines, Iowa, where Doughten and Thompson lived, on a budget of about $60,000, and it was promoted only by word of mouth. Its success exceeded their wildest expectations. At the peak of its popularity, Mark IV was booking 1,500 rentals per month. Some local libraries held as many as fifteen copies

FIGURE 9.2. Left-behind heroine, Patty, waking up alone in a postrapture world, *A Thief in the Night*, 1972/3.

in order to keep up with the demand from churches and other organizations. Many groups, including my own youth group, rented it regularly—for annual Halloween or New Year's Eve showings, for example.

In all, *Thief* generated more than $1 million, an unprecedented amount in rental revenues. By 1984, including video tape sales, it had reportedly grossed $4.2 million. Estimates as to how many people have seen the film range from one hundred million to an astounding three hundred million viewers.[8]

Given those numbers, it is not surprising that the movie had a tremendous influence on innumerable American teens. It literally scared the hell out of many, who started getting themselves ready by converting at the end of the movie. In fact, Doughten and Thompson had this effect in mind: in one scene, a little girl who is terrified of being left behind without her mom says a very simple, scripted prayer to ask Jesus into her heart, thereby providing viewers with the words they need for their own conversion prayers. Still, other traumatized youth ran the other way. Satanic rock performance artist Marilyn Manson, for example, recalls being terrified by the movie, which ultimately helped push him in a more Nietzschian beyond-good-and-evil direction.[9]

Thief also had tremendous influence on the emergence of evangelical horror as a genre of film aimed at scaring people into conversion. Not only did its financial success pave the way for Mark IV's sequels (*A Distant Thunder* in 1977, *Image of the Beast* in 1981, and *Prodigal Planet* in 1983), but it also opened the door to other kinds of Christian B-movie horror, most notably the hellfire-and-real-maggots splatter films about what happens to you in hell by Ron and June Ormond, who converted to Christianity after cutting their teeth making sexploitation movies in the 1960s. Some of their best-known movies, like *The Burning Hell* (1974) and *The Grim Reaper* (1976), sent overwhelmed viewers running from church basement screenings to throw up and/or cry and/or get saved.

A Thief in the Night of the Living Dead

Part of what distinguishes *A Thief in the Night* from later, far more violent and often more expensive evangelical horror films is the weirdly slow-paced, downhome Iowa,

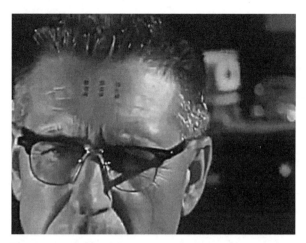

FIGURE 9.3. Close-up forehead of a UNITE citizen with the binary computer readout of 666, "the Mark of the Beast," *A Thief in the Night*, 1972/3.

low-fidelity banality that drives its vision of a postrapture world in the aftermath of God.

Some of this lo-fi vibe was unintentional. Doughten and Thompson were working with a very small budget. The actors were all local Des Moinesians with little or no experience in the film industry. Even the Fishmarket Combo, which performed the movie's theme song, "I Wish We'd All Been Ready," was a local group of Young Life student volunteers. There was no money to create cinematic spectacles of crashing planes and trains, people being swept up into the heavens, and demonic world leaders marking the foreheads of frightened lefts-behind.

In fact, the scene depicting the actual moment of rapture does not take place until more than halfway through the movie and marks the time shift from Patty's prerapture flashbacks to her terrifying postrapture, left-behind world. The scene itself is eerily dull: a series of cuts between the lead singer of the Fishmarket Combo mowing his suburban lawn and a lonely little puff cloud in the sky. The last cut is to the lawnmower, now unmanned but still running in the middle of the tree lawn.

Oddly effective, this little puff cloud was not what Doughten and Thompson were shooting for. They wanted theophanic thunderclouds to depict the dramatic scene of Christ's return to claim his own. Throughout the shooting of the film, however, there were no clouds in the Des Moines sky. Thompson happened to have some saved footage of a single cloud, and they were left with that as their only option.

However unintended, the dreariness of this scene fits perfectly with the rest of this lo-fi Des Moinesian rapture tale. When the one-world government organization UNITE institutes its mark to indicate conformity with their rule, we see elderly locals sitting at card tables politely smiling and pointing to their hands or foreheads to indicate where they would prefer to take it.

In many respects, the film is reminiscent of other early low-budget, lo-fi horror movies from the 1960s and 1970s. Take, for example, the scene immediately following the opening performance, in which a series of quick cuts between shaky handheld shots of carnival images in saturated color is accompanied by a soundtrack of oddly demonic funhouse laughter created by sound director Ralph Carmichael, who has sometimes been called the

"Bernard Herrmann of Christian cinema"—Herrmann being best known for the screeching violins in Alfred Hitchcock's 1960 horror movie, *Psycho*.[10]

Much of what lends *A Thief in the Night* this lo-fi vibe of the end-times banality that remains after God's departure is particularly reminiscent of George Romero's lo-fi *Night of the Living Dead* from 1968. Production-wise, both films were shot in bland urban environments (*Night* in Pittsburgh, Pennsylvania, and *Thief* in Des Moines, Iowa) on low budgets ($114,000 for *Night* and $60,000 for *Thief*), both used mostly nonprofessional and first-time actors, and both films are grainy with generally poor, hollow sound quality.

Beyond these similarities in quality and production, the two films also share several narrative elements. Both, for example, use emergency radio and television broadcasts in order to provide viewers with the broader, global context of the personal and local crisis. In fact, both movies begin with a radio suddenly turning on by itself: a car radio in *Night* and Patty's bedside radio in *Thief*.

Most strikingly living-dead like, however, are the scenes related to Patty's arrest by UNITE, her escape, and the ensuing chase through the strangely empty city and nearby woods: first, as Patty sits alone in her darkened house at night, watching the news, while zombie-like UNITE police lurk outside; then, after her arrest and escape, as she keeps easily slipping away from her slow, speechless, easily eluded but ultimately relentless pursuers, especially when, at one point, she stumbles in horror into a zombie-like elderly couple with marked foreheads.

At the same time, the movie is very effective in encouraging viewers to identify with Patty, who by the middle of the movie is the only character who has been left behind without taking the mark. (Her liberal pastor, Reverend Turner, played by Doughten himself, was also left behind, but, after renouncing his former liberal theology and resisting UNITE, he was executed.) Two common film strategies work together to create this identification with Patty in her postrapture, God-forsaken isolation.

First is the long, dreamlike series of flashbacks that explain what has happened, namely that the saved have been raptured. These flashbacks include a sermonette by the lead singer of the Fishmarket Combo warning of the coming rapture; sermons by and conversations with the good pastor (as opposed to the liberal pastor) that explicate the rapture and tribulation to come and explain how to be saved by accepting Jesus Christ as one's personal lord and savior; a video montage of pictures of Patty and her husband's first few months of happy marriage before the rapture, overlaid with a mournful instrumental version of the movie's theme song, "I Wish We'd All Been Ready"; and the conversions of Patty's husband and one of Patty's friends who, along with God, have left her behind.

The second means of encouraging identification with Patty is the film's use of shot/reverse-shot sequences. These involve an initial shot facing a character looking at someone or something, immediately followed by a shot turned roughly 180 degrees around, so that viewers see what that character sees (often followed by a third shot that returns to the original point of view). The effect of such sequences is to identify the subjectivity of the viewer with that of the character in the first shot.

There are several shot/reverse-shot sequences in *Thief* that build viewer identification with Patty in her alienation from everyone and everything else. During the flashback scenes, they often involve Patty reacting in disbelief and doubt to the good pastor or to her husband's accepting of his gospel message. In other cases, they involve Patty confronting and evading UNITE's thugs and zombie-like old people who have taken the mark. With each of these shot/reverse-shots, the world of the viewer, like that of Patty, grows more hostile and isolating. Until, trapped by her former friends, she jumps off a bridge, presumably to her death, only to awake to her alarm and find herself exactly where the whole thing started, left behind.

Encrypting Revelation

The cryptic placement of Revelation-related mythemes within the movie's broader pretribulation rapture narrative also contributes to its disturbing lo-fi horror vibe. There are three places in particular where bits of Revelation encrypt themselves within the film.

The first and most obvious is the use of the computer-generated number 666 as the mark people must take to show their submission to and alliance with UNITE. Oddly, the number is never explicitly identified as the number of the mark of the beast of Revelation, which his minions must take on their right hand or forehead in order to be able to buy or sell (Revelation 13:16–18). Nor is UNITE ever explicitly linked to the beast or its demonic dominion over the God-forsaken earth. These undeciphered symbols leave Patty, and most of the viewers identifying with her, inexplicably uncertain and in the dark.

The second Revelation mytheme derives from the armored locusts with human faces that are released to torture those who do not have the seal of God on their foreheads (Revelation 9:1–11). In an early scene, a shot from below of a helicopter taking off fades into a close-up shot of a grasshopper on a kitchen window. Perplexing to many viewers, this visual association of helicopter and grasshopper is a reference to the belief, popular among end-times enthusiasts in the early 1970s, that the locusts John *thought* he saw were actually Cobra attack helicopters that would be part of the future battle of Armageddon. Later in the movie, Patty is chased by UNITE soldiers flying the same helicopter.[11]

The third element from Revelation encrypted in the film is the warning that Christ will return "like a thief in the night" (Revelation 3:3 and 16:15; see also 1 Thessalonians 5:2).[12] Having become so commonplace in evangelical discourse, this idea is usually taken simply to mean that it will happen when you least expect it. But placed in the context of this movie, a more horrifying, if largely sublimated, sense emerges, namely, an image of the divine as a threatening figure who could, at any moment, invade your home and steal you or, worse, your loved ones—which is exactly what happens to Patty, as she awakens to find her husband's electric shaver buzzing in the sink.

Combine these film strategies with the ritual context in which the film was typically experienced—as part of a captive congregation of young people in a Christian youth group meeting, opened and closed in prayer, in the evening, in a church or similar religious space—and you might even prefer it were the night of the living dead instead of the day after the rapture.

From Rapture Horror to Rapture Adventure

Others have traced the rather dull but lucrative path from *Thief* through the many rapture and tribulation movies and video shorts of the 1980s and 1990s that led to Cloud Ten Pictures' *Left Behind* movies, all based more or less on the best-selling series of apocalyptic fantasy-action novels by Tim LaHaye and Jerry B. Jenkins: first, the trilogy (*Left Behind: The Movie* in 2000; *Left Behind II: Tribulation Force* in 2002; and *Left Behind III: World at War* in 2005); and then in the single *Left Behind* movie starring Nicolas Cage in 2014.[13]

As the title "left behind" suggests, and as authors La-Haye and Jenkins readily acknowledge, their series drew much inspiration from *A Thief in the Night* and its sequels. Indeed, there is not a lot that is both new and interesting in the *Left Behind* movies (or the books for that matter). They are chock-full of now stock images and motifs from the evangelical apocalyptic mythosphere, drawn from early dispensationalist diagrams, Baptista's early rapture film, and, of course, *A Thief in the Night*. There are the now-expected unmanned planes, trains, and automobiles crashing into each other; weeping mothers, clutching baby blankets and teddy bears of raptured children; wifeless husbands and husbandless wives; pets lingering over the clothes of raptured masters (apparently babies and young children go but pets do not); and, of course, remorseful liberal pastors left behind in their chapels, only realizing that they betrayed their faith once it was too late.

And yet, although cinematographically unremarkable, the *Left Behind* trilogy and the most recent *Left Behind* redux with Nicolas Cage are worth our attention as symptoms of the changing face of evangelical apocalyptic culture. They signal a shift away from the *horror* and toward the *thrill*. In them, apocalyptic dread has become apocalyptic anticipation.

In *A Thief in the Night*, being left behind really was a living nightmare, abandoned in a creepily dull, God-forsaken Iowa wasteland. There the withdrawal of God highlights the absence of loved ones, and the withdrawal of loved ones highlights the absence of God.

In the *Left Behind* movies, on the other hand, as in the novels and video game, the postrapture world of those left behind is where all the action is.[14] Here we have an apocalyptic thriller, as our heroes, the "tribulation saints," lead the ultimate resistance movement against the ultimate bad guy, the Antichrist, Nicolae Carpathia, whose name and Bela-Legosi-like accent suggest that he is intended to represent a sort of evil descendent of Bram

Stoker's original diabolical invader from the Carpathian Mountains. In these movies, unlike in *Thief*, we almost feel badly for the ones who got raptured. They are missing out on all the excitement.

Cloud Ten clearly intended to produce sequels to their 2014 release starring Nicolas Cage. In the last shot of that film, one of the main characters gazes on the city skyline in flames, shakes his head and says, "It looks like the end of the world." To which another responds, "No, not yet. I'm afraid this is just the beginning." Alas, Cloud Ten does not appear to have found sufficient underwriting or grassroots funding to make another *Left Behind* movie. Its Indiegogo .com fundraising campaign failed miserably, reaching only 16 percent of its goal of $500,000 before closing in May of 2015. Indiegogo's standard notification of the campaign's end, "No Time Left," rang with peculiar irony.

From Rapture Adventure to Zombie Apocalypse

In the wake of the latest *Left Behind* flop, Cloud Ten's co-founder Paul Lalonde has discovered something new to do with his time. He has left behind the Christian Revelation-inspired rapture story world inaugurated by *A Thief in the Night* for another end-times cultural treasure trove—indeed the very one conjured by *Night of the Living Dead*: zombies.

In the spring of 2016, it was announced that Lalonde, Michael Walker, and John Vidette of Back 40 Pictures will be producing a remake of David Cronenberg's 1977 sci-fi zombie thriller, *Rabid*, which is about a woman who, after undergoing plastic surgery, develops a taste for human blood, turning her victims into bloodthirsty zombies who in turn infect others.

The movie will be directed by the twin sister team of Jen and Sylvia Soska, who were to begin shooting in early 2018.[15] The Soska sisters are best known for horror flicks like *American Mary* (2012), about a young woman who pays her way through medical school by working with clients from the extreme body modification community, and *Dead Hooker in a Trunk* (2009), about a night gone bad that begins with "Badass" and "Geek," played by Jen and Silvia Soska themselves, picking up their friend "Goody Two Shoes" from a church youth group meeting.

No doubt this new film venture confirms what the authors of the *Left Behind* books, Tim LaHaye and Jerry Jenkins, had strongly suspected after their film rights battles with Cloud Ten: that Lalonde is more Nicolae Carpathian than tribulation saint. But I doubt Lalonde cares. He is following the money. Rapture movies seem to be played out, at least for time being, whereas zombie culture is still trending.

That said, the postrapture story world has more in common with the zombie story world than one might initially think. I suggest five points of comparison that might begin to draw tribulation saints and zombie hunters closer together.

First, both story worlds emerge in some sense after God, in the wake of divine presence, in the theological vacuum of a perceived withdrawal of God from the world. They are story worlds of God-forsakenness, living hells.

Second, both story worlds are built on a dynamic of us-versus-them. The "us" is a community of individual souls under siege, still conscious of what is going on and trying to save themselves. The "them" are those undifferentiated, unindividuated, brainwashed or braindead masses who have already been lost to the forces of evil and living deadness. The monstrous threat of "them" outside to "us" inside is above all the threat of losing one's individual subjectivity—literally losing one's soul. In the postrapture world, Patty and we viewers who identify with her risk losing our souls under the pressure to conform to the dominant order of UNITE, whose very name signifies the homogeneous subordinated oneness of its marked subjects. Similarly, in the zombie-infested story world, the survivors and we viewers who identify with them risk losing our souls under a relentless deluge of unindividuated, mindless bodies, an entropic heat bath of animated death.[16]

Third, both story worlds are constructed to scare the hell out of us. Imagining myself in the evangelical postrapture story world, I am terrified into denouncing the powers of evil and accepting Jesus Christ as my personal Lord and savior. Imagining myself in the world of zombies, I am compelled to pull close to my companions, to build a safe and secure community against the forces of chaos impinging on all sides (think gated communities and "Homeland Security"). In both scenarios, those on the outside are already lost and forsaken, and their lostness and forsakenness is experienced as a direct threat to my power to remain among the living, in the Book of Life.

Fourth, both story worlds are especially popular in times of war, terrorism, and mass death. Is it an accident that Baptista's rapture movie was released during World War II? Or that both *A Thief in the Night* (as well as Hal Lindsey's *The Late, Great Planet Earth*) and *Night of the Living Dead* came out during the Vietnam War and in the context of escalating Soviet-American Cold War tensions? Or that the second rounds of both have come out during the American "war on terrorism" in the wake of September 11, 2001? The story worlds of raptures and zombies give expression to the collective trauma of meaningless mass violence and death—and so did John's Revelation in its first-century context, as we discussed previously.

Fifth and finally, not only do both story worlds resonate with the war-tornness of Revelation, but both draw literally from elements of it. We have already seen in detail how Revelation figures into rapture horror culture. But it is also an inspiration to zombie horror culture, most notably in its description of people seeking death but not finding it ("death will flee from them"; Revelation 9:6) and its description of the so-called "first resurrection" (Revelation 20), in which the dead who had not taken the mark and had been beheaded are brought back to life. As the devout Christian Hershel Greene from the popular television series *The Walking Dead* puts it while zombies are about to take over his farm and family, "I can't profess to understand God's plan. Christ promised the resurrection of the dead. I just thought he had something a little different in mind."[17]

The Horror

Taken together with the rapture and tribulation themes in evangelical apocalyptic horror movies, this zombie connection testifies to the variety of ways that Revelation feeds into deep, largely repressed correspondences between religion and horror in contemporary culture. Whereas the postrapture story world dwells on the fear of being left behind, in the time of tribulation and in the wake of divine presence, zombies climbing out of their graves speak to the mostly sublimated sense of horror and repulsion at the Christian vision of the resurrection of the dead (however tamed through their glorification), a vision drawn largely from the Revelation tradition and made a central tenet of Christian faith in the Nicene Creed, which proclaims belief in the bodily resurrection of the dead.

As reanimations of Revelation, rapture horror and zombie apocalypse share something we have seen again and again in this biography of Revelation: a fascination with its horror and violence that trumps the beauty of its final vision of a new heaven, new earth, and shiny new Jerusalem where the righteous live happily ever after with God and Christ. Why is that? Why does the horror and violence in the middle so overshadow the joy and peace in the end? Perhaps, despite its overwhelming, even unimaginable atrocities, many of us find a world filled with such terrors more believable than a world without them.

Post Script

Revelation Becomes Us

There is a certain nostalgia to this series on "Lives of Great Religious Books." It is no accident that they are being published, as lovely print books, in the twilight years of print book culture. Not that print books are going away; but they will never again be the dominant, taken-for-granted medium for reading and writing. Ours is a time of looking back appreciatively on the lives of books in the era of print.

But Revelation has never rested comfortably under the covers of a print book. Yes, there is a text tradition that we call the "book" of Revelation, strings of written words, heard and read, cohering around sequences of sevens into something of a loose narrative arc that leads finally to a vision of the last battle, Last Judgment, and the coming of a new heaven, new earth, and new holy city. Yet even that text tradition has lived as many different media, from early Christians reading aloud to handwritten scrolls to codices to illuminated manuscripts to print books to audio recordings, software, and mobile web applications. As we have seen throughout this biography, moreover, those words keep pulling away from each other into new literary and verbal contexts, endlessly combining with other images, music, spaces, and things. Revelation is not a book, not even narrowly a text, but an ever expanding and contracting multimedia constellation.

Revelation becomes us. Its loose arc of images and phrases, bits and pieces expand and contract within our imaginations, ever spinning off into new revelations, new diagrams of history, new decipherments of geopolitics, new worlds of unfamiliar gods, new stagings of epiphany, new fantasies of rapture, new nightmares of being left behind. And, ironically enough, there is no end in sight. Revelation continues to thrive in and through proliferation. We could point to hundreds of recent reanimations of it— from television shows to movies to songs to websites to new religious movements—each one drawing from and adding to it. Some show evidence of at least some familiarity with the text of the biblical book of Revelation, while many others do not. Such post-Christian, postbiblical lives of Revelation testify to its potential to outlive even the religious tradition that canonized it in the first place.

We Are in Apocalypse

"Revelation does not carry its warning on its label," biblical scholar Stephen D. Moore writes.

> It is only when we have devoured the book, avidly read it right through, that we learn that its seal was always already broken. Revelation is an unsealed book.

Toxic poisons trickle from it. Consciousness-altering fumes waft out of it. Desperate hope and vindictive joy issue from it.[1]

Is it still necessary to read it, "right through," for its poisons, fumes, hopes, and joys to find their ways into us?

"The world was fucked up many years ago, as you know," said a young man on his phone a few seats in front of me on the Cleveland Red Line to the airport. "We've been living in the book of Revelation." I looked up from the book I was reading, feminist theologian Catherine Keller's *Apocalypse Now and Then*, and thought, Keller would agree.[2]

"We are in apocalypse," she writes. "We are in it as a script that we enact habitually when we find ourselves at an edge, and we are in it as recipients of the history of social and environmental effects of that script."[3] Behind this "apocalypse script" is a basic "apocalypse pattern" built from certain elements of Revelation, namely:

a proclivity to think and feel in polarities of "good" versus "evil"; to identify with the good and to purge the evil from oneself and one's world once and for all, demanding undivided unity before "the enemy"; to feel that the good is getting victimized by the evil, which is diabolically overpowering; to expect some cataclysmic showdown in which, despite tremendous collateral damage (the destruction of the world as we know it), good must triumph in the near future with the help of some transcendent power and live forever after in a fundamentally new world.[4]

Insofar as this imagined ultimate purging of evil from good is fundamentally impossible in lived experience, moreover, our apocalypse scripts encourage us to see ourselves as the faithful in a time of oppression, subjected to the powers of evil. These powers take many forms, as we have seen, from the "kingdom of darkness," as our yoga-wary friends might put it, to a diabolical papacy, as Cranach depicted it.

Drawn from pieces of Revelation (diabolically evil enemies, ecological cataclysm, impending final battle and Last Judgment), the apocalypse script is simultaneously our situation and our interpretation of our situation. We perform it, and it in turn interprets our performance. It is a feedback loop of self-fulfilling prophecy.

We are of course familiar with this habit among the Christian right, enraptured as it is with rapture theory to the point that it can disregard our very real potential to wear out our welcome on the planet because we will not need it for much longer. We are also familiar with the many websites and chain emails during Barak Obama's two terms as president of the United States purporting to prove that he was the Antichrist. Likewise, Hillary Clinton has been believed by many on the right to be the whore of Babylon ever since she began work on universal health care in 1993 during her husband Bill Clinton's presidency.

On the other hand, President Donald J. Trump's formal recognition of Jerusalem as the capital of Israel in December of 2017 has been celebrated by many apocalyptically oriented Christian conservatives as a fulfillment of biblical prophecy, setting the scene for the Second Coming of Christ and his reign in Jerusalem. As

Matthew Gabrielle aptly observes, such interpretations of Trump's decision locate it "within sacred, rather than secular time," making it "part of God's plan for the world, a step on the way to the reunification of the holy city (still considered occupied under international law) and the restoration of the ancient Israelite Temple. In other words, a step on the way towards the apocalypse."[5]

But those on the left, religious and nonreligious alike, are also habituated to the apocalypse script, even decrying those very leaders on the right in terms of Revelation, projecting on them diabolically evil powers of deception and inhuman violence, and linking their lies to the worldly pursuit of wealth at the expense of the poor and the oppressed. Since Trump's election in November of 2016, many have linked him to the beast of Revelation and the number 666, noting, among other portents, that his election year, 2016, is the sum of $666 + 666 + 666 + 6 + 6 + 6$; that he frequently makes an "okay" hand sign that forms the number six; and that his son-in-law Jared Kushner's real estate company owns 666 Fifth Avenue in New York.[6]

More serious signs of a rise in apocalyptic anxiety on the left are the growing numbers of liberals devoted to preparing for a doomsday event—a terrorist attack, for example, or a civil war incited by white nationalists fomented by Trump and his administrative plans (e.g., repealing the Affordable Care Act, increasing nuclear capabilities, etc.). The Liberal Prepper, for example, is a closed Facebook group for progressives, started on election night 2016. Its nearly four thousand members share strategies for preparing for an apocalyptic disaster, including tutorials on canning vegetables, building bunkers, and finding alternative energy sources in order to learn to live off the grid.[7] I joined, mainly for research purposes, but I must admit that my Alaska upbringing during the Cold War years endears me to such buggers-out. On my last visit to the page, the banner was a painting of two people wearing gas masks (children? mother and child? husband and wife?) posing in front of their log cabin in the woods. A recent well-liked post included a snapshot from a bookstore of a sign explaining that "Post Apocalyptic Fiction has been moved to our CURRENT AFFAIRS section." The one who shared it added the comment, "Kinda funny . . . until it isn't."

Indeed, the apocalypse script can be as habit-forming in post-Christian and anti-Christian culture as it is among Christians. Consider the hit song, "American Woman," first released by Canadian rock band The Guess Who in 1970 at the height of Vietnam War protests and covered many times since, most recently by Lenny Kravitz.[8] "American woman, I said get away," the singer warns. Describing her hypnotizing the masses with colored lights, he shuns her advances. "I don't need your war machines . . . your ghetto scenes." This woman is a misogynistic personification of American imperialism, superficially attractive but ultimately deadly, seducing the world into unjust wars and oppression. She is a revamp of Revelation's whore of Babylon. The deep irony here is that the real addiction we cannot shake is not this sexist personification of the seductress "American woman" as embodiment of ultimate evil. The real addiction is to the apocalypse script that drives that personification.

Even the legendary heavy metal band Black Sabbath, alleged by its Christian critics to be Satanic, could not help but take a hit from the apocalypse script in their "War Pigs," also released in 1970.[9] "Now in darkness world stops turning," lead singer Ozzy Osborne announces, "Ashes where the bodies burning." As the sun goes dark while the bodies still smolder, divine judgment has dawned. "Day of judgment, God is calling," while the war pigs crawl on their knees, begging for mercy for their sins—but no mercy comes. "Satan laughing spreads his wings," gathering the former masters of war and ushering them into eternal torment.

Whenever we construct a world in which we see ourselves as real or potential victims of diabolical powers, we are performing the apocalypse script. Whenever we promote our enemies to the status of cosmic evil in opposition to all that is good in the world, we are performing the apocalypse script. It embeds itself in our perceptions of the world like lines of code copied and pasted into our cultural programming, iterating history into demonizing loops of a "good" us versus an "evil" other.

Heads or Tails

I believe there is another side to this apocalypse script. Indeed, it is the other side of the same coin. We might call it the *dominion script*. It is our equally addictive delusional faith in our own godlike dominion and immortality as a species.

This other script, this heads-side of the coin, also has roots in the Christian Bible, but at the other end: "Be fruitful and multiply, and fill the earth and subdue it; and have dominion over the fish of the sea and over the birds of the air and over every living thing that moves upon the earth" (Genesis 1:28). A blessing and charge to humankind, made in the image of God, to multiply, fill, subdue, and dominate.

Such was the biblical benediction of Western capitalism—its "charter foundation," as Francis Bacon called it. Under its banner, science, technology, and economic growth marched forth to reclaim humankind's Edenic status of godlike dominion over the rest of creation. Under it, Western European explorers and entrepreneurs marched into Africa and Asia, justifying global expansion, the expropriation of land, and the enslavement of indigenous peoples that drove the early, preindustrial era of war capitalism.[10] We may hear this blessing's echo still today in futurists proclaiming that, through science and technology, we will soon engineer our way out of our own mortality and ultimately deny death's sting, as if we are the gods now.

When our delusions of dominion fail us, when we come face to face with our very ungodlike fleshly vulnerability and finitude, the apocalypse script is our habitual go-to. Rather than accepting, indeed living the truth of our mortality as a species, we instead turn apocalyptic. We project our own finality onto the world. The world is going to hell in a hand basket. "The world was fucked up many years ago," as my fellow commuter put it. The end is near, too late to change course. Moreover, those responsible for this mess are the embodiment of ultimate evil. Our only hope is a bailout from God, including brand-new bodies and a brand-new heaven and earth to replace the ones we trashed.

Dominion and apocalypse are two sides of the same coin, a coin minted in the modern West that now has currency everywhere that has been touched by the West in its long history of colonialism, Christian mission, and global capitalism. Heads or tails, both work to deny our ultimate belonging to this world, which we imagine we will either dominate or leave. Or dominate and then leave. Both scripts work to deny the humility of our own humanity, which, like the word itself, is bound to the humus, the ground.

How to get off this dime?

A good start might be to go back and read some more Bible, to reread the texts that form the scriptural core of these delusions. Despite rapture theory, for example, the book of Revelation is clearly a very this-worldly text, envisioning the ultimate renewal or recreation of this world, not escape to another. This is consistent with other New Testament traditions, including the teachings of Jesus, which imagine the coming "kingdom of God" not as an otherworldly realm for God and humans but as an earthly kingdom.

The image in Genesis 1 of humankind as godlike subduers and dominators of the earth is likewise undermined by closer reading. Just a few verses later, we find a decidedly counterdominionist story of human beginnings. There, the human is quite literally an "earth creature":

God creates the first human (Hebrew *ha'adam*) by breathing life into the earth (*ha'adamah*). The human comes from humus and, when it breathes its last, returns to it. Formed from dirt and animated by divine breath, the earth creature is made to "serve" (*'abad*) and "keep" (*shamar*) the earth (Genesis 2:7, 15). God creates animals the same way, meaning that they, too, are literally spiritual, divinely inspired earth creatures, as intimately close to God as they are to the ground (2:19).

Like so many biblical ideas, the dominion and apocalypse scripts work best when they keep their distance from the scriptures they claim as their origins. These days that distance is easy to maintain. After all, biblical literacy is at an all-time low, even among so-called Bible believers.[11] The truth is that biblical ideas and values are rarely literally biblical, and these two scripts are no exception. Having detached from their biblical contexts centuries ago, they have become theological scripts for the rise of modern capitalism.

Going Forth

The apocalypse script is but one life of Revelation thriving in the world today. Like its other lives, past and present, it begins by breaking off from its larger narrative contexts and attaching itself to a new horizon of meaning. The break leaves a rough, porous surface that readily bonds with other surfaces, allowing the formation of new conglomerations, new monstrous forms.

Revelation's birth was indeed a monstrous one: not created *ex nihilo* or even from dust, but stitched together, like Dr. Frankenstein's monster, from various bits and pieces of Jewish scriptures and other mythologies, and then brought to life in some obscure, dark corner of the early Jesus movement that is now lost to us.

Soon this monstrous life became many lives, as pieces of it broke off and took hold in new contexts and new media environments, to the point now that its biography is in some sense *our* biography. We are in Revelation and Revelation is in us.

In her introduction to the 1831 republication of her novel *Frankenstein*, Mary Shelley famously wrote, "And now, once again, I bid my hideous progeny go forth and prosper."[12] Did she mean her book or its monster? No doubt both. For *Frankenstein* the novel, like Revelation, is monstrous, a reincarnation and reanimation of elements from various mythic figures, giving birth to a homunculus who rails against his creator with the passion and eloquence of Job. And now, as we have seen, the lives of both Frankenstein and Revelation are much more, indeed something other than, their literary text traditions. They are multimedia phenomena, known and shared by many who have never read a word of writing about them.

Whether or not Mary Shelley could have imagined her book and her monster going forth and prospering into the twenty-first century, John of Patmos certainly could not have. Do we dare bid this hideous progeny continue to go forth and prosper? Whether or not we do, it will.

COMMENTARIES AND CRITICAL STUDIES

Aune, David. *Revelation.* Word Biblical Commentary. 3 vols. Dallas: Word, 1997–98.

Barr, David L. *Tales of the End: A Narrative Commentary on the Book of Revelation.* Santa Rosa, CA: Polebridge, 1998.

Beale, G. K. *The Book of Revelation: A Commentary on the Greek Text.* New International Greek Testament Commentary. Grand Rapids, MI: Eerdmans, 1999.

Blount, Brian K. *Revelation: A Commentary.* New Testament Library. Louisville, KY: Westminster/John Knox, 2009.

Frillingos, Christopher A. *Spectacles of Empire: Monsters, Martyrs, and the Book of Revelation.* Philadelphia: University of Pennsylvania Press, 2004.

Garrow, A. J. *Revelation.* New Testament Readings. New York: Routledge, 1997.

Huber, Lynn R. *Like a Bride Adorned: Reading Metaphor in John's Apocalypse.* New York: T & T Clark, 2007.

Kampen, John. "The Genre and Function of Apocalyptic Literature in the African American Experience." In *Text and Experience: Towards a Cultural Exegesis of the Bible,* edited by Daniel Smith-Christopher, 43–65. Sheffield: Sheffield Academic Press, 1995.

Koester, Craig A. *Revelation: A New Translation with Introduction and Commentary*. Anchor Yale Bible Commentaries. New Haven, CT: Yale University Press, 2014.

Levine, Amy Jill, with Maria Mayo Robbins, eds. *A Feminist Companion to the Apocalypse of John*. New York: Continuum, 2009.

Malina, Bruce J., and John J. Pilch. *Social-Science Commentary on the Book of Revelation*. Minneapolis, MN: Fortress, 2000.

Moore, Stephen D. *Empire and Apocalypse: Postcolonialism and the New Testament*. Bible in the Modern World 12. Sheffield: Sheffield Phoenix Press, 2006.

———. *Untold Tales from the Book of Revelation: Sex and Gender, Empire and Ecology*. Resources for Biblical Study 79. Atlanta: Society of Biblical Literature Press, 2014.

Pagels, Elaine. *Revelations: Visions, Prophecy, and Politics in the Book of Revelation*. New York: Viking, 2012.

Perkins, Pheme. *The Book of Revelation*. Collegeville Bible Commentary 11. Collegeville, MN: Liturgical Press, 1983.

Pippin, Tina. *Death and Desire: The Rhetoric of Gender in the Apocalypse of John*. Literary Currents in Biblical Interpretation. Louisville, KY: Westminster/John Knox Press, 1992.

Rowland, Christopher. *Revelation*. Epworth Commentaries. London: Epworth, 1993.

Schüssler Fiorenza, Elizabeth. "Apocalypsis and Propheteia: Revelation in the Context of Early Christian Prophecy." In *L'Apocalypse Johannique et l'apocalyptique dans le Nouveau Testament*, edited by J. Lambrecht, 105–28. Glembloux: J. Duculot, 1980.

———. *The Book of Revelation: Justice and Judgment.* 2nd ed. Minneapolis, MN: Fortress, 1998.

Wall, Robert W. *Revelation.* New International Biblical Commentary. Peabody, MA: Hendrickson Publishers, 1991.

Witherington, Ben, III. *Revelation.* New Cambridge Bible Commentary. Cambridge: Cambridge University Press, 2003.

CULTURAL AND RECEPTION HISTORY

Backus, Irena. *Reformation Readings of the Apocalypse: Geneva, Zurich, and Wittenberg.* Oxford: Oxford University Press, 2000.

Blount, Brian K. *Can I Get a Witness? Reading Revelation through African American Culture.* Louisville, KY: Westminster, 2005.

Boesak, Allan A. *Comfort and Protest: The Apocalypse from a South African Perspective.* Philadelphia: Westminster, 1987.

Bynum, Caroline Walker, and Paul Freedman, eds. *Last Things: Death and the Apocalypse in the Middle Ages.* Philadelphia: University of Pennsylvania Press, 1999.

Chilton, Bruce. *Visions of the Apocalypse: Receptions of John's Revelation in Western Imagination.* Waco, TX: Baylor University Press, 2013.

Emmerson, Richard K., and Bernard McGinn, eds. *The Apocalypse in the Middle Ages.* Ithaca, NY: Cornell University Press.

Keller, Catherine. *God and Power: Counter-Apocalyptic Journeys.* Minneapolis, MN: Fortress, 2005.

Kovaks, Judith, and Christopher Rowland. *Revelation.* Blackwell Bible Commentaries. Oxford: Blackwell, 2004.

Rhoads, David, ed. *From Every People and Nation: The Book of Revelation in Intercultural Perspective*. Minneapolis, MN: Fortress, 2005.

Richard, Pablo. *Apocalypse: A People's Commentary on the Book of Revelation*. Maryknoll, NY: Orbis, 1995.

Sánchez, David A. *From Patmos to the Barrio: Subverting Imperial Myths*. Minneapolis, MN: Fortress, 2008.

Wright, Ben, and Zachary W. Dresser, eds. *Apocalypse and the Millennium in the American Civil War Era*. Baton Rouge: Louisiana State University Press, 2013.

APOCALYPTICISM

Boyer, Paul S. *When Time Shall Be No More: Prophecy Belief in Modern American Culture*. Cambridge, MA: Harvard University Press, 1992.

Cohn, Norman. *The Pursuit of the Millennium: Revolutionary Millenarians and Mystical Anarchists of the Middle Ages*. Revised and expanded edition. New York: Oxford University Press, 1971.

Collins, Adela Yarbro. *Cosmology and Eschatology in Jewish and Christian Apocalypticism*. Leiden: Brill, 2000.

———. *Crisis and Catharsis: The Power of the Apocalypse*. Philadelphia: Westminster, 1984.

Collins, John J. *The Apocalyptic Imagination: An Introduction to the Jewish Matrix of Christianity*. New York: Crossroad, 1984.

Frykholm, Amy. *Rapture Culture: Left Behind in Evangelical America*. New York: Oxford University Press, 2004.

Hanson, Paul D. *The Dawn of Apocalyptic: The Historical and Sociological Roots of Jewish Apocalyptic Eschatology*. Revised edition. Minneapolis: Fortress, 1979.

Keller, Catherine. *Apocalypse Now and Then: A Feminist Guide to the End of the World*. Boston: Beacon, 1996.

McGinn, Bernard. *Apocalyptic Spirituality: Treatises and Letters of Lactantius, Adso of Montier-en-Der, Joachim of Fiore, the Spiritual Franciscans, Salvanarola*. Classics of Western Spirituality. Mahwah, NJ: Paulist Press, 1979.

Murphy, Kelly J., and Justin Jeffcoat Schedtler, eds. *Apocalypses in Context: Apocalyptic Currents through History*. Minneapolis, MN: Fortress, 2016.

ACKNOWLEDGMENTS

Spending a few years with the Apocalypse of John has been unnerving enough; writing its biography has been almost too much. In the course of following it through so many historical contexts beyond my academic expertise, Revelation's nightmare visions of falling stars and cosmic blood baths have for me often blurred into more tangible, professional nightmares of trying to say something meaningful, maybe even insightful, hopefully not embarrassing, in scholarly fields where I have little right to say much of anything at all. It has been a humbling experience, as my footnotes only begin to attest, and I gladly acknowledge my tremendous debt to scholars in those fields where I have tread; I have learned a great deal from them, and I hope that I have done justice to their remarkable work.

I am grateful for the support of a Public Scholars Award from the National Endowment for the Humanities, which afforded me a good six months of full-time devotion to researching and writing this book.

While on my NEH leave, I also started a new life of commuting between Cleveland, Ohio, and Denver, Colorado. The commute has not been easy, but patient support from Case Western Reserve University and new colleagues in Denver have helped a great deal. Many thanks to my writing group at Iliff School of Theology, namely Pamela Eisenbaum, Mark George, and Ted Vial, who not only worked their way through my first draft but also helped me work my way through the anonymous reader reports on that manuscript, offering many invaluable suggestions for revision along the way. And many thanks to Greg Robbins, who hosted me as Marsico Visiting Professor at the University of Denver, who welcomed me into his seminar, who offered essential guidance in navigating Eusebius and Irenaeus, and who gave me the amazing little book on "the 666 System" with which I begin my preface. And heartfelt gratitude to Michael Hemenway, who joined me in a months-long staged writing race—a tour of sorts—the rules for which were too complicated to describe here except to say that a lot of words got written and a lot of bourbon got drunk.

Thanks to many other colleagues who helped in many essential ways: Tod Linafelt, Colleen Conway, Bill Deal, Robert Spadoni, Peter Knox, Kelly Murphy, Emory Yarnton, and, as always, members of the Tel Mac Theory Lunch and Praxis Breakfast group. Thanks, too, to my mother, Geraldine Beal, who read the full first draft, made others read it, and encouraged me do my best to make it more worth reading.

Thanks for institutional and administrative support and encouragement from my department's administrative assistant, Lauren Gallitto, and from my dean, Cyrus Taylor, fan of the Grateful Dead's cover of Blind Willie

Johnson's "John the Revelator" if not of Revelation itself. Thanks to Chancellor Rebecca Chopp for research privileges at the University of Denver, and to Patrick Graham at Emory University's Pitts Theological Library for guided access to its wonderful archives.

I have benefited tremendously from opportunities to share my work in progress: a keynote at the annual meeting of the Southeastern Commission for the Study of Religion in Atlanta, Georgia; a keynote at the conference "Constructing Bible and Jesus in Contemporary Culture" at the University of Agder in Kristiansand, Norway; an invited lecture at the conference "Protestantism on Screen: Religion, Politics, and Aesthetics in European and American Movies" at Martin Luther University of Halle-Wittenberg, Germany; a Marsico Lecture at the University of Denver; and, above all, weekly discussions with undergraduate students in my seminar on Revelation at Case Western Reserve University.

Special thanks to my editor, Fred Appel, for patience, support, and engaging conversation; to editorial assistant Thalia Leaf for keeping the whole process moving forward efficiently and smartly; and to the two anonymous readers, whose sometimes quite critical concerns and substantive recommendations for revision have, I believe, made for a better book.

Thanks to the cafes and diners where I like to write, and to the people working in them who are fine with me doing so over coffee, breakfast specials, and tacos: Annie's, St. Mark's, Illegal Pete's, Cake Crumb, The Corner Beet, and especially Tommy's. Thanks, too, to the places where I write while I fly back and forth between Denver and Cleveland, especially seats 7A and 7F.

Deep gratitude to the late John Gibson, an alumnus of Case Western Reserve University and a distinguished professor emeritus of Tufts University, who took interest in this project early on, engaged me in lively conversation, and supported my research, making possible a trip to the original site of the monastery of Joachim of Fiore in the Calabrian mountains of southern Italy.

Finally, and as ever, deep thanks to Clover Reuter Beal for steadfast encouragement, loving engagement, and a decidedly unapocalpytic perspective on what really matters.

PREFACE

1. Mary Stewart Relfe, *When Your Money Fails: The "666 System" Is Here* (Montgomery, AL: Ministries, Inc., 1981), 15–20.

2. Relfe, 21–22. By referring to John as a "fisherman," Relfe indicates that she believes the author of Revelation is John the brother of James and son of Zebedee. See the forthcoming discussion of authorship.

3. Hal Lindsey, *The Late, Great Planet Earth* (Grand Rapids, MI: Zondervan, 1970). See the discussion of *A Thief in the Night* and Larry Norman's song in the context of that film in chapter 8. An excellent historical study of the persistence of such apocalyptic "prophecy belief" in American popular culture, focusing especially on the 1970s and 1980s, is Paul S. Boyer, *When Time Shall Be No More: Prophecy Belief in Modern American Culture* (Cambridge, MA: Harvard University Press, 1992).

4. "The Reagans: First Family Easing into Private Life," *Los Angeles Times*, November 19, 1988.

5. Tony Allen-Mills, "Mothers Expect Damien on 6/6/06," *The Sunday Times*, April 30, 2006, http://www.thesundaytimes.co.uk/sto/news/uk_news/article200645.ece. "Damien" refers to the adopted

child Damien Thorn in *The Omen* film trilogy (1976–81) who turns out to be the Antichrist.

6. Eric Sondheimer, "Kentucky Cross Country Runner Forfeits Rather Than Wear No. 666," *Los Angeles Times*, November 6, 2013, http://articles.latimes.com /2013/nov/06/sports/la-sp-vi-kentucky-cross-country -runner-forfeits-rather-than-wear-no-666-20131106.

7. Laura Barron-Lopez, "Representative Avoids Apocalyptic 666," *The Hill*, February 4, 2015, http://thehill .com/policy/energy-environment/231787-republican -avoids-apocalyptic-666.

8. For readers interested in a more comprehensive cultural and social history of Revelation, I recommend consulting my suggestions for further reading. Included there are several masterful reference works that I myself have found indispensable in my own more selective research. I am especially indebted to the works of Kovacs and Rowland, Blount, and Keller.

CHAPTER I. INTRODUCTION

1. The Greek noun *apokalupsis*, which later Christian tradition used to name this originally untitled text, derives from the Greek *apo*, "from" or "out of," plus *kalupto*, "to cover" or "veil." Although most scholars call the text the Apocalypse of John, most English Bibles call it Revelation. This title comes from the postclassical Latin *revelationem*, related to the verb *revelare*, which, like *apokalupto*, describes removing a covering or veil: *re*, "un-" or "back," as in returning to an original state, plus *velare*, "to veil" or "cover." Still, in Revelation 1:1, the Latin Vulgate text uses the

Greek term *apokalupsis* rather than its Latin synonym *revelationem*.

2. Elisabeth Schüssler Fiorenza, *Revelation: Justice and Judgment*, 2ⁿᵈ ed. (Minneapolis, MN: Fortress, 1998); Tina Pippin, *Death and Desire: The Rhetoric of Gender in the Apocalypse of John*, Literary Currents in Biblical Interpretation (Louisville, KY: Westminster John Knox, 1992); Pippin, *Apocalyptic Bodies: The Biblical End of the World in Text and Image* (London and New York: Routledge, 1999); and Caroline Vander Stichele, "Re-membering the Whore: The Fate of Babylon According to Revelation 17:16," in *A Feminist Companion to the Apocalypse of John*, ed. Amy-Jill Levine with Maria Mayo Robbins (New York: T&T Clark, 2009), 106–20. As Stephen D. Moore, *Untold Tales from the Book of Revelation: Sex and Gender, Empire and Ecology* (Atlanta: Society of Biblical Literature, 2014), 5–6, notes, queer theory has found fruitful ground in Revelation, first, because it includes characters performing sex acts (2:10–22; 14:8; 17:1–2; 18:3; 19:2), but also, more significantly, because it includes so many examples of nonheteronormativity: "Revelation also has a Jesus with female breasts ('girt about the paps [*tois mastois*] with a golden girdle' [1:13], as the King James translators matter-of-factly put it); a choir of 144,000 male virgins (14:1–4); a bride whose groom is a sheep (19:7–9; 21:9); and other arresting deviations from standard sex/gender scripts, whether ancient or modern."

3. The main precursor to this approach is biblical reception history, which explores the history of the reception of biblical texts, images, stories, and characters

through the centuries in the form of citation, interpretation, reading, revision, adaptation, and influence.
On what I believe are inherent limitations of biblical
reception history, see my "Reception History and
Beyond: Toward the Cultural History of Scriptures,"
Biblical Interpretation 19 (2011): 357–72. I hasten to
point out that many scholars whose work goes by
biblical reception history have already moved beyond
that approach into what I would consider cultural
history. See esp. Brennan W. Breed, *Nomadic Text: A
Theory of Biblical Reception History* (Bloomington: In-
diana University Press); and Colleen M. Conway, *Sex
and Slaughter in the Tent of Jael: A Cultural History of
a Biblical Story* (New York: Oxford University Press,
2016), who approaches the cultural history of the Jael
narrative in Judges in terms of cultural "performances"
rather than "productions" as a means of attending to
the "capacities of this particular story to do or mean
certain things at different moments in history."

4. We might think of these story-shaped images as something like *memes*, a term coined by Richard Dawkins
in *The Selfish Gene* (Oxford: Oxford University Press,
1976; revised 2016) as a cultural analogue to genes
(drawing the word from the Greek *mimeme*, something imitated, but abbreviated to sound like "gene").
Dawkins described the meme as "a unit of cultural
transmission, or a unit of imitation. . . . Examples of
memes are tunes, ideas, catch-phrases, clothes fashions,
ways of making pots or of building arches" (249).
Yet my interests diverge from much of what goes
by "memetics" today in two significant ways. First,
memetics shows little explicit interest in the centrality

of media in the circulation of memes within culture. Second, and relatedly, the primary focus of memetics is the spread of competing ideas and beliefs—the epidemiology of ideas through replication-as-imitation—in the process of cultural evolution (e.g., Douglas R. Hofstadter, "On Viral Sentences and Self-Replicating Structures," in *Metamagical Themas: Questing for the Essence of Mind and Pattern* [New York: Basic Books, 1985]; Aaron Lynch, *Thought Contagion: How Belief Spreads Through Society* [New York: Basic Books, 2008]; and Susan Blackmore, *The Meme Machine* [Oxford: Oxford University Press, 1999]). I share an interest in the evolutionary dimensions of how these units survive through mutation and reproduction. How, that is, has this weird biblical tradition managed to survive and thrive? I think it has a lot to do with these portable, adaptable, mutable, story-shaped memes. However, my interest in this question is not restricted solely to the spread of competing ideas and beliefs. Indeed, as we will see, many of the story-shaped images of Revelation carry almost no epistemological or ideological content.

5. In 1:18, Papyrus 98 omits the phrase *kai ho zōn*, "and the living," that appears in most other manuscripts. On Oxyrhynchus Papyrus 115, see Bruce M. Metzger and Bart D. Ehrman, *The Text of the New Testament: Its Transmission, Corruption, and Restoration*, 4th ed. (New York: Oxford University Press, 2005), 61. A helpful summary of the manuscript evidence for Revelation is in Brian K. Blount, *Revelation: A Commentary*, New Testament Library (Louisville, KY: Westminster John Knox, 2009), 22–26. For a fuller

discussion of the main differences among manuscripts see Bruce M. Metzger, *A Textual Commentary on the Greek New Testament*, corrected ed. (London: United Bible Societies, 1975), 729–67. The problem of the absence of an "original" text of Revelation is an instance of the general problem of the absence of originals for any New Testament texts. For a helpful discussion, see esp. David Parker, *The Living Text of the Gospels* (Cambridge: Cambridge University Press, 1997), which shows how such a hypothetical original of Jesus's sayings on divorce in the synoptic Gospels quickly deconstructs under closer text-critical scrutiny. The definitive scholarly statement on the problematic idea of an original text for the New Testament is Eldon Epp, "The Multivalence of the Term 'Original Text' in the New Testament Textual Criticism," *Harvard Theological Review* 92.3 (1999): 245–81.

6. See esp. Michael Hemenway, *Bible as Interface* (PhD dissertation, University of Denver and Iliff School of Theology, 2017). See also the kindred approach to Revelation by Tat-Siong Benny Liew, *What Is Asian American Biblical Hermeneutics?: Reading the New Testament* (Honolulu: University of Hawaii Press, 2008), 134: "I do not want to reinforce the power of the origin(al), as if the origin(al)—in this case, the book of Revelation—had an essence that, once identified, should and/or could dictate everything that comes afterward. . . . I want to enlarge the 'canon' not (only) of the Bible but of biblical studies."

7. Except where noted, translations are from the New Revised Standard Version (NRSV), National Council of the Churches of Christ, 1989. My own comments

on and occasional translations of the Greek text are based on the twenty-seventh edition of the Nestle-Aland *Novum Testamentum Graece*, edited by Barbara and Kurt Aland (Stuttgart: Deutsche Bibelgesellschaft, 1993).

8. On the metaphorical language of veiling and unveiling vis-à-vis gender, sexuality, and sexual identity in Revelation as it relates to ancient contexts of bridal imagery, see esp. Lynn R. Huber, *Like a Bride Adorned: Reading Metaphor in John's Apocalypse*, Emory Studies in Early Christianity (New York: T & T Clark, 2007), 179–84, where John's announcement of his text as an *apokalypsis*, as "unveiling," anticipates the climactic gendered *anakalypsis*, also "unveiling," of the bride in Revelation 20. See also her *Thinking and Seeing with Women in Revelation* (London: Bloomsbury, 2013).

9. Note that the words translated in 1:2 as "testified" (*emarturesen*) and "testimony" (*marturian*) also carry the sense of martyrdom and suffering (see 6:9, 12:17, and 20:4). Perhaps John's use here suggests a linkage between witnessing or testifying and suffering or martyrdom.

10. The Greek verb *eidon*, "I saw" or "looked" is used throughout the text as a simple transition from one vision to the next (also, less frequently, *ekousa*, "I heard" or "listened"). Most translations, including the NRSV, alternate between "I looked" and "I saw," presumably to avoid the seeming awkward repetitiveness in the Greek text. In my retelling here, I am translating the verb consistently as "I saw" in order to highlight this repetition, which I see as key to the text's rhetorical effect of overwhelming readers and hearers.

11. There are no references outside Revelation to these figures of Balaam, Jezebel, or the Nicolaitans as enemies of the faith. Jezebel likely harkens back to the northern Israelite Queen Jezebel, wife of King Ahab, who was criticized by the prophet Elijah for hosting prophets of Baal and Asherah as well as Yahweh (1 Kings 16–2 Kings 9) and for killing the prophets of Yahweh. Her life ended in violent murder at the command of the rival to the northern throne, Jehu. Although Revelation sexualizes her as a fornicating temptress, no such image of her is found in the Hebrew biblical narrative; she is straightforwardly a very forceful queen (in contrast to her weak and impressionable husband King Ahab) and theological archenemy of Elijah. Perhaps John's reference to Balaam similarly harkens back to the Hebrew biblical story of Balaam, a prophet and diviner caught between the Israelites and their enemies, the Moabites, in Numbers 22–24. In that story, Balak, the king of Moab, hires Balaam to curse the Israelite armies, but God intervenes, essentially reversing Balak's plans, which leads to a defeat of the Moabites. The Nikolaitans, unknown outside of Revelation, may simply refer to followers of someone named Nicolaus (i.e., Nicholas), perhaps the one who was among the seven elected leaders of the early Jesus movement in Jerusalem (Acts 6:5). By the late second century, beginning as far as we know with Irenaeus's *Against Heresies* (c. 180 CE), the Nicolaitans are explicitly linked to that Nicolaus.

12. On this text's misogynistic sexualization of the other, set against the idealizing objectification of Jerusalem as the bride, see esp. Pippin, *Death and Desire*.

13. Maia Kotrosits, "Seeing Is Feeling: Revelation's Enthroned Lamb and Ancient Visual Affects," *Biblical Interpretation* 22 (2014): 478, 485.

CHAPTER 2. PALE RIDER: OBSCURE ORIGINS

1. The most compelling argument for dating Revelation to the end of the Jewish wars (specifically 69 CE) is John W. Marshall, *Parables of War: Reading John's Jewish Apocalypse* (Waterloo, Canada: Wilfrid Laurier University Press, 2001), esp. 88ff. Marshall also argues—convincingly, to my mind—that Revelation be understood as a Jewish rather than a Christian document, based primarily on its invectives against the "synagogue of Satan," its emphasis on keeping commandments, its vision of the army of 144,000 drawn from the tribes of Israel, and its vision of the destruction and return of the holy city of Jerusalem. See also Marshall, "Collateral Damage: Jesus and Jezebel in the Jewish War," in *Violence in the New Testament*, ed. Shelley Matthews and E. Leigh Gibson (London: T & T Clark, 2005), 35–50; and note 18 of this chapter.

2. Philo of Alexandria, *On the Embassy to Gaius*, 11–15, offers Philo's firsthand account of going to Caligula. Cassius Dio's *Roman History*, 59.26–28, mentions that Caligula sometimes referred to himself as Jupiter in public documents and reveals that he had the heads of other gods removed from some temples and replaced with castings of his own. See also Michael Farquhar, *A Treasure of Royal Scandals* (New York: Penguin Books, 2001).

3. See Philo's summary of the anti-Jewish persecutions in *Flaccus*, 9.58–72. Leonard Victor Rutgers, "Roman

Policy toward the Jews: Expulsions from the City of Rome during the First Century CE," in *Judaism and Christianity in First Century Rome* (Eugene, OR: Wipf and Stock, 1998), 96 and 114–16, points out that there never was a "once-and-for-all" standard Roman policy with regard to Jewish religious practices and observances. On the questionable credibility of Josephus's discussion in his *Antiquities* of senatorial decrees regarding the Jews in Rome, see H. Moehring, "The Acta pro Judaeis in the Antiquities of Flavius Josephus," in *Christianity, Judaism, and Other Greco-Roman Cults*, ed. Jacob Neusner (Leiden: Brill, 1975), 124–58.

4. Josephus, *The Wars of the Jews*, 2.14.5, in *The Works of Flavius Josephus*, trans. William Whiston (Auburn and Buffalo, NY: John E. Beardsley, 1895); available online, along with the Greek edition of Benedictus Niese, *De bello Judaico*, at http://www.perseus.tufts.edu. An excellent discussion of the value of Josephus's works for understanding the history and theological contours of ancient Judaism into the first century CE is Jonathan Klawans, *Josephus and the Theologies of Ancient Judaism* (New York: Oxford University Press, 2012).

5. Josephus, *Wars of the Jews*, 2.14.9.

6. Ibid., 2.17.6 (Whiston's translation of ἐπεὶ δὲ τὰ νεῦρα τῆς πόλεως καταφλέξαντες).

7. Cassius Dio, *Roman History*, 66.6.

8. Klawans, *Josephus and the Theologies of Ancient Judaism*, 17–18, rightly cautions against treating this crisis as something closer to an unbearable and uninterpretable trauma, noting that many who have done so implicitly compare it to the Holocaust. Indeed,

as Klawans shows, Josephus's own account develops a theological perspective on this crisis that is drawn from his earlier theological reflections on the destruction of the First Temple in 587 BCE. I am persuaded by Marshall, *Parables of War*, that this is the proper context in which to understand the theological-interpretive work of Revelation as well.

9. Pliny the Younger's *Panegyricus*, delivered to the Senate in 100 CE in honor of Emperor Trajan, contrasts the ease with which citizens approached Trajan against the terror of approaching the monstrous and unpredictable Domitian, who he says murdered relatives and plotted the massacres of good citizens.

10. Eusebius, *Ecclesiastical History*, 3.17–18. He quotes Irenaeus, *Against Heresies* 5.30.3, in *Ecclesiastical History*, 3.18.3. The context of Irenaeus's comment is a discussion of whether the number 666 referred to a particular emperor. Had it been necessary to know, Irenaeus writes, then John, writing toward the end of Domitian's reign, would have specified.

11. Blount helpfully summarizes the two main arguments from internal evidence (that is, evidence within the text of Revelation itself) for dating the writing to the time of Domitian. First is its practice of referring to Rome as Babylon, thus implicitly linking the destruction of the Second Temple in 70 CE to the fall of Jerusalem and the destruction of the First Temple in 587 BCE. It is certainly conceivable, however, that such a connection would have been made *during* the Jewish rebellion, before the temple's ultimate destruction. The second piece of internal evidence for the later dating relates to John's references to the beast returning

from the dead (ch. 13 and 17). Against some scholars who take these texts as evidence of an earlier dating of the book, treating them as allusions to the legend that Emperor Nero (d. 66 CE) would return from the dead to take vengeance on the Roman west that had spurned him, David Aune argues that, although this legend is attested as early as 69 CE, it did not achieve "widespread currency" until much later (*Revelation* [Dallas: Word Press, 1997], 1:lxix–lxx; cited in Blount, 8). The old argument, which used external evidence for the later dating, was based on the belief promoted by early Roman historians and Christians like Irenaeus and Eusebius that Domitian was an especially severe persecutor of Christians and Jews—a belief that historians today reject, as Blount makes clear.

12. Justin Martyr, *Dialogue with Trypho*, ch. 81.

13. Irenaeus, *Against Heresies*, 4.20.11.

14. Eusebius, *Ecclesiastical History*, 3.39. For an assessment of later datings of Papias's writings to around 130 CE, and an argument for an earlier date range of 95–100 CE, see Robert W. Yarbrough, "The Date of Papias: A Reassessment," *Journal of the Evangelical Theological Society* 26 (1983): 81–91.

15. Eusebius, *Ecclesiastical History*, 7.25.1–2.

16. Ibid., 7.25.6–27.

17. Pamela Eisenbaum, *Paul Was Not a Christian: The Original Message of a Misunderstood Apostle* (San Francisco: HarperOne, 2009), 6–7. Indeed, as Eisenbaum points out, some scholars argue that Christians did not "materially distinguish themselves" from mainstream Roman culture until the late third or early fourth century.

18. David Frankfurter, "Jews or Not? Reconstructing the 'Other' in Rev 2:9 and 3:9," *Harvard Theological Review* 94 (2001): 403–25, argues convincingly that those "who say they are Jews and are not" are not Jews outside the Jesus movement but rather "a constituency *within* the Jesus movement who were claiming the label 'Jew' in a manner that John finds illegitimate. This constituency . . . embraces Pauline and neo-Pauline proselytes to the Jesus movement who were not, in John's eyes (nor in many others' in the first century), halakhically pure enough to merit this term in its practical sense" (403). On these references to a "synagogue of Satan" as evidence for identifying Revelation as a Jewish text, see Marshall, *Parables of War*, 12–16. Marshall identifies a long history of anti-Jewish rhetoric of Christian supersessionism, going back to the fourth-century Victorinus, bishop of Petau, who interprets those "who say they are Jews and are not" as Jews who reject Christ.

19. Elaine Pagels, *Revelations: Visions, Prophecy, and Politics in the Book of Revelation* (New York: Viking, 2012), 54.

20. G. K. Beale, *John's Use of the Old Testament in Revelation*, The Library of New Testament Studies 166 (London: Bloomsbury T & T Clark, 2015).

21. Julia Kristeva, "Word, Dialogue and the Novel," in *Desire in Language: A Semiotic Approach to Literature and Art*, ed. Leon Roudiez (New York: Columbia University Press, 1980), 65–66. See also Kristeva, *Revolution in Poetic Language*, abridged ed., trans. M. Waller (New York: Columbia University Press, 1984), 60.

CHAPTER 3. APOCALYPSE NOT NOW:
AUGUSTINE'S TALE OF TWO CITIES

1. Eusebius, *Ecclesiastical History*, 8.6.9.

2. Ibid., 8.4.2

3. Elaine Pagels, *Revelations: Visions, Prophecy, and Politics in the Book of Revelation* (New York: Viking, 2012), 133ff.

4. Athanasius, *Arian History*, 22, in *The Nicene and Post-Nicene Fathers of the Christian Church*. Vol. 4, *Select Writings and Letters of Athanasius, Bishop of Alexandria*, ed. Philip Schaff and Henry Wace (Grand Rapids: Christian Classics Ethereal Library, 2005); compare Revelation 17:3–4, 18:6. See also the fuller discussion in Pagels, *Revelations*, 141–44.

5. Athanasius, *Festal Letter*, 39.6, in *Nicene and Post-Nicene Fathers*, Schaff and Wace; compare Revelation 22:18–19: "I warn everyone who hears the words of the prophecy of this book: if anyone adds to them, God will add to that person the plagues described in this book; if anyone takes away from the words of the book of this prophecy, God will take away that person's share in the tree of life and in the holy city, which are described in this book."

6. *The Confessions of Saint Augustine*, trans. Edward B. Pusey, in *The Nicene and Post-Nicene Fathers of the Christian Church*, ed. Philip Schaff (Grand Rapids, MI: Christian Classics Ethereal Library, 2005), 1:6.15.

7. Ibid., 9.6.

8. Garry Wills, *Augustine's Confessions: A Biography* (Princeton, NJ: Princeton University Press, 2011), 8.

9. Paula Fredriksen, "Tyconius and Augustine on the Apocalypse," in *The Apocalypse in the Middle Ages*, ed. Richard K. Emmerson and Bernard McGinn (Ithaca, NY: Cornell University Press, 1992), 31.

10. Augustine's interpretation did not emerge *ex nihilo*. A key influence on him was Tyconius, a Donatist (a movement rooted in Diocletian's persecutions that advocated extremely rigorous, saint-like perfection) from the late decades of the fourth century whose commentary on Revelation has not survived. For a thorough discussion of him as central precursor to Augustine, see Fredriksen, "Tyconius and Augustine."

11. Augustine, *The City of God*, trans. Marcus Dods, in *Nicene and Post-Nicene Fathers of the Christian Church*, ed. Philip Schaff (Edinburgh: T & T Clark), 2:13.1. Augustine's discussion of the two cities, the two resurrections, the Second Coming, and the Last Judgment are all in the second half of the work, Books 11–22. Subsequent references to and quotations of passages from this work are cited parenthetically.

12. The latter part of *City of God*, Book 20 (chapters 18–30) focuses on integrating other biblical texts believed to be about the Antichrist (false messiah) and Last Judgment into this reading of Revelation (e.g., 2 Peter and 1–2 Thessalonians as well as Daniel, Psalms, Isaiah, and Malachi). Book 21 then focuses on the punishment of the wicked, that is, the end of the second city.

13. For a fascinating study of the heavenly books motif in early Jewish and Christian apocalyptic literature, see Leslie Baynes, *The Heavenly Book Motif in Judeo-Christian Apocalypses 200 BCE–200 CE* (Leiden: Brill, 2012). Augustine's explication of the book of life

not as a literal book but as a divine power that will instantaneously make all things known may be seen as an innovation on earlier scenes in which such heavenly books were handled by angels or exalted scribes.

CHAPTER 4. CRY OUT AND WRITE: HILDEGARD'S APOCALYPSE

1. On the burgeoning of apocalyptic spirituality in the late Middle Ages, during which scenes from Revelation intermix with fragments from many other prophetic and apocalyptic texts, see Bernard McGinn, *Apocalyptic Spirituality: Treatises and Letters of Lactantius, Adso of Montier-en-Der, Joachim of Fiore, the Spiritual Franciscans, Salvanarola*, Classics of Western Spirituality (Mahwah, NJ: Paulist Press, 1979), all translated and introduced by McGinn.

2. E.g., Frederick Barbarossa, King of Germany and Holy Roman Emperor, who in 1159 appointed Victor IV as "antipope" against Pope Alexander III.

3. For an excellent discussion of this Christian prophetic social milieu, see especially the introduction in Margaret Reeves, *The Influence of Prophecy in the Later Middle Ages: A Study in Joachimism* (Oxford: Oxford University Press, 1969).

4. As Norman Cohn, *The Pursuit of the Millennium: Revolutionary Millenarians and Mystical Anarchists of the Middle Ages*, rev. and exp. ed. (New York and Oxford: Oxford University Press, 1971), 14–15, writes, "Throughout the Middle Ages the Sibylline eschatology persisted alongside the eschatologies derived from the Book of Revelation, modifying them and being modified by them but generally surpassing them in

popularity. For, uncanonical and unorthodox though they were, the Sibyllines had enormous influence—indeed save for the Bible and the works of the Fathers they were probably the most influential writings known to medieval Europe."

5. In another prophetic oracle, the fourth-century writing known as the *Tiburtine Sibyl*, a pagan sibyl prophesies that the Western Roman Emperor Constans, son of Constantine and opponent of the Arian heresy who was assassinated in 350 CE, will be raised from the dead to rule Rome and usher in Christ's eternal reign. Arian theology saw Christ as the first of all creation but not one with the creator God. It was rejected at the Council of Nicaea (325 CE).

6. On Hildegard and Joachim as meliorists, see Kathryn Kerby-Fulton, "Prophet and Reformer: 'Smoke in the Vineyard,'" in *Voice of the Living Light: Hildegard of Bingen and Her World*, ed. Barbara Newman (Berkeley: University of California Press, 1998). For an excellent biography of Hildegard, see esp. Barbara Newman, "'Sybil of the Rhine': Hildegard's Life and Times," in the same volume, to which this brief discussion owes a great deal.

7. *Hildegard of Bingen: Scivias*, trans. Mother Columbia Hart and Jane Bishop, The Classics of Western Spirituality (New York: Paulist Press, 1990), prologue. All quotations of *Scivias* are from this translation and edition, in consultation with the 1513 Latin text printed by Jacques Lefevre d'Etaples and published in J.-P. Migne, ed., *Sanctae Hildegardis abbatissae Opera omnia*, Patrologiae cursus completus, series latina 197 (Paris, 1855).

8. This Rupertsberg codex was lost in Dresden during World War II. A black-and-white photocopy of it survives, along with a full-color hand copy by the nuns at Eibingen and illustrated by Dame Josepha Knips (1927 to 1933). Images reproduced here are from this hand copy.

9. Ibid.

10. Oliver Sacks, *The Man Who Mistook His Wife for a Hat* (New York: Simon & Schuster, 1970), 169, acknowledging the earlier argument of Charles Singer in 1917, "The Visions of Hildegard of Bingen," rev. ed. in 1928; reprinted in *Yale Journal of Biology and Medicine* 78 (2005): 57–82.

11. Carolyn Walker Bynum, "Preface," in *Scivias*, 4.

12. Anne Clark, "Hildegard of Bingen," *The Oxford Encyclopedia of the Bible and the Arts*, ed. Timothy Beal (New York: Oxford University Press, 2015), 433. Extra-biblical writings were part of this process as well. They probably included Augustine, Ambrose, Gregory the Great, and Bede, among others. As Clark writes, "Hildegard's respect for this commentarial tradition shines forth in her vision of the word of God, symbolized by a three-sided column representing the Old Testament, the New Testament, and 'the unhusking (*enucleationem* or "exposition") of the faithful doctors' (*Scivias* III, 4.5)" (431).

13. *Scivias*, prologue.

14. Hildegard uses the longer phrase, *Post haec vidi et ecce*, at the opening of visions 3, 5, and 12 of Book 3. She uses the shorter phrase, *Post haec vidi*, in visions 3 and 5 of Book 1; visions 3, 5, and 6 of Book 2; and visions 6 and 9 of Book 3. Although neither phrase appears

anywhere else in the Vulgate canons of the Old and New Testaments, each appears once in 2 Esdras (13:8 and 12).

15. Hildegard calls this diabolical dragon *serpentem antiquum* in *Scivias* 2.6 and 7 (and *serpentis antiqui* in 3.1 and 2). The identical phrase appears in the Vulgate text of Revelation 20:2 (and *serpens antiquus* in 12:9). Nowhere else in the Vulgate Bible is Satan called an "ancient serpent." In both texts, this nomenclature is deployed in the context of the dragon being chained to the abyss so that it can no longer deceive the nations.

16. Here and elsewhere, the titles given for each of the books, visions, and subjects within each vision are not Hildegard's but are provided by Hart and Bishop to help organize the text and orient readers.

17. Vision 11 also draws from and innovates on that of Adso of Moutier-en-Der, *De ortu et tempore Antichristi*, ed. D. Verhelst, CCCM 45; English translation by John Wright in his appendix to *The Play of Antichrist* (Toronto: Pontifical Institute of Mediaeval Studies, 1967).

18. Barbara J. Newman, "Introduction," in *Scivias*, 43.

19. On Gebeno and Hildegard, see Kathryn Kerby-Fulton, *Reformist Apocalypticism and Piers Plowman* (Cambridge: Cambridge University Press, 1990), 29–31; and "Gebeno of Eberbach and the Consequences," Land der Hildegard, landderhildegard.de/fascination /history-of-reception. On the history of reception of Hildegard's works via Gebeno and other pseude-pigraphal works, see Michael Embach, *Die Schriften Hildegards von Bingen. Studien zur ihrer Überlieferung*

*und Rezeption im Mittelalter und in der Frühen
Neuzeit* (Berlin: De Gruyter, 2003).

20. On the survival of textual traditions, as livings-
beyond, in conversation with Walter Benjamin on
translation as survival, see esp. Tod Linafelt, *Surviving
Lamentations: Catastrophe, Lament, and Protest in
the Afterlife of a Biblical Book* (Chicago: University of
Chicago Press, 2000).

CHAPTER 5. MIND'S EYE:
JOACHIM IN THE FORESTS OF HISTORY

1. Excellent sources for Joachim's biography and his
systematics include Bernard McGinn, *Apocalyptic
Spirituality: Treatises and Letters of Lactantius, Adso
of Montier-en-Der, Joachim of Fiore, the Spiritual
Franciscans, Salvanarola*, Classics of Western Spiri-
tuality (Mahwah, NJ: Paulist Press, 1979), 97–148;
Marjorie Reeves, *The Influence of Prophecy in the Later
Middle Ages: A Study in Joachimism* (Oxford: Oxford
University Press, 1969); and Marjorie Reeves and B.
Hirsch-Reich, *The Figurae of Joachim of Fiore* (Oxford:
Oxford University Press, 1972).

2. Reeves and Hirsch-Reich, *Figurae*, 20–21, make clear
that "to use *figurae* was with him a habitual method"
from early on in his work. That such figures were original to his actual publications in his three major works
is supported by the fact that they are "embedded in the
text of all three major works[, which] sets it beyond
doubt that Joachim himself drew figures to teach his
disciples and readers." Reeves and Hirsch-Reich discuss
all the most complete copies that include figures
(Oxford, Reggio, and Dresden manuscripts) along with

fragments and pseudo-Joachimist collections of figures. As indicated in their tables, xxi–xxiii, the figures of the dragon and the tables of concords that I discuss later in this chapter are in all the complete manuscripts and several of the fragments and pseudo-Joachimist mansucripts. See also excerpts translated from manuscripts by McGinn, *Apocalyptic Spirituality*, 113–48. The images of the Reggio manuscript of the *Liber Figurarum* can be seen, along with transcription keys, at http://www.centrostudigioachimiti.it/Gioacchino /GF_Tavole.asp#. The 1527 Venice edition of Joachim's *Exposition on the Apocalypse* is available via Google Books at https://books.google.com/books?id= 1BvsdZhz64MC. A critical edition of the Latin text of the *Enchiridion super Apocalypsim*, which was a briefer introduction to his understanding of the Apocalypse of John (and which may have been included with his *Exposition* as the "Liber introductorius" in the edition he sent to the Holy See for approval), is Edward Kilian Berger, ed., *Enchiridion super Apocalypsim* (Toronto: Pontifical Institute of Mediaeval Studies, 1986).

3. Reeves, *Influence of Prophecy in the Later Middle Ages*, 3. The *Catalogus* is available on Google Books at https://books.google.com/books?id= 5sE5AAAAcAAJ&source=gbs_navlinks_s.

4. Dante, *Paradiso*, 12.140–41.

5. McGinn, *Apocalyptic Spirituality*, 100.

6. Joachim, *Exposition*, folio 39 verso. The Latin text, as transcribed by Reeves, *Influence of Prophecy in the Later Middle Ages*, 22, is as follows: "*subito mihi meditanti aliquid, quadam mentis oculis intelligentie claritate percepta de plenitudine libri huius et tota*

veteris ac novi testamenti concordia revelatio facta est."
Thanks to colleague Peter Knox for translation advice.

7. John himself had drawn from this same vision in his
own scene of the four living creatures in the throne
room of heaven (Revelation 4:6–8). John did not,
however, incorporate the earthly wheels within
wheels to which the creatures are intimately linked in
Ezekiel's vision. Moreover, whereas each of Ezekiel's
four creatures has one animal face, each of John's four
creatures has four different faces pointing in different
directions.

8. Quotations here are from *Enchiridion* 10–11 (Berger,
Enchiridion super Apocalypsim, 19–20; cf. "Liber
introductorius" in the *Exposition* 2r–3v), an overview
of his larger exposition of Revelation, as translated and
discussed in Randolph Daniel, "Joachim of Fiore: Patterns of History in the Apocalypse," in *The Apocalypse
in the Middle Ages*, ed. Richard Kenneth Emmerson
and Bernard McGinn (Ithaca, NY: Cornell University
Press, 1992), 78–79.

9. Sources for Joachim's decoding of the seven-headed
dragon include his "Introduction" (10 recto to 11 recto)
in his *Exposition*, his extended commentary on the
verses of Revelation 12 in the *Exposition* itself (156 recto
to 156 verso; 196 recto to 197 recto), and the image and
captioning in *Liber Figurarum* (Reggio edition; translated in McGinn, *Apocalyptic Spirituality*, 136–41).

10. My suggestion to think of scriptural "users" rather
than "readers" is from Michael Hemenway, *Bible as
Interface* (PhD dissertation, University of Denver and
Iliff School of Theology, 2017), who argues convincingly for this reconception, which highlights the

broader variety of interactivities involved in scriptural practices within manuscript codex culture as much as within print book culture and emerging new media.

11. Both the "sea monster" (*tannin*) and Leviathan are consistently translated as *drakon* ("dragon") in the Septuagint (Greek) version of the Old Testament. See, e.g., Ezekiel 29:3, in which the "great sea monster" (Hebrew *hattannim haggadol*) is translated into Greek as "the great dragon" (*ton drakonta ton megan*), whom God will "cast down" (*katabalo*, from the verb *ballo*, "cast"). Resonating with this image from Ezekiel, Revelation twice refers to the red dragon as "the great dragon" (*ho drakon ho megas* in 12:9; also 12:3) and describes him being "cast out" (*eblethe*, also from *ballo*) of heaven by God (12:9). In the Septuagint text of Psalm 74:12-14, furthermore, both Leviathan and the "sea monster" (*tannin*) are translated into Greek as *drakon*. This psalm describes the dragon with multiple heads (*tas kephalas tou drakontos*, "the dragon's heads"), as does Revelation 12:3 (*tas kephalas outou*, "his heads"). The Septuagint text of Isaiah 27:1 also translates both Leviathan and the "sea monster" (*tannin*), whom God will kill on a future day of judgment, as *drakon*. The Hebrew proper name Leviathan is also translated into Greek as *drakon* in Psalm 104 (LXX 103) and Job 41. See also Timothy Beal, *Religion and Its Monsters* (New York: Routledge, 2001), 71–85.

12. All translations of the text in *Liber Figurarum* are from McGinn, *Apocalyptic Spirituality*, 136–41. See also McGinn's notes to this text, 294–96.

13. McGinn, *Apocalyptic Spirituality*, 194, notes that, in the context of other works, Joachim identifies some of

the horns (though not the first three or the sixth) with different persecutors.

14. Ibid., 138.
15. Reeves and Hirsch-Reich, *Figurae*, 151–52.
16. Ibid., 21.
17. Ibid., 40–51. Reeves and Hirsch-Reich argue convincingly that Joachim's literary-visual reading of the Alpha and Omega in Revelation 1:8 in his *Expositio* precedes the fuller visual explication in his *Figurae*, supporting my point that the focused analysis of this text is core to the larger diagramming of the Trinity.
18. Joachim makes the same substitution in his *Expositio* on Revelation 1:8 (34r–34v).
19. This "veil" in Hebrew is *masveh*, "cover" or "sheath"; in the Greek Septuagint it is *kalumma*, "covering," related to *apokalupto*; in the Latin Vulgate it is *velum*, related to *revelare*.
20. See also 1 Corinthians 13:12, another of Joachim's favorite passages: "Now we see in a mirror, dimly, but then we will see face to face. Now I know only in part; then I will know fully, even as I have been fully known."
21. See the subsequent fuller discussion of dispensationalism and its influence on James Hampton's throne room.

CHAPTER 6. SEPTEMBER'S TESTAMENT:
LUTHER'S BIBLE VS. CRANACH'S REVELATION

1. The sheer size and weight of whole-Bible codices was also a practical challenge to keeping the canon closed. The oldest surviving whole Vulgate Bible, the eighth-century Codex Amiatinus, is twenty inches high, a little over thirteen inches wide, more than seven inches thick, has over two thousand pages, and weighs

about seventy-five pounds. For more on Jerome, the Vulgate, and canonical history, see Timothy Beal, *The Rise and Fall of the Bible: The Unexpected History of an Accidental Book* (New York: Houghton Mifflin Harcourt, 2011), 117–20.

2. For a fuller discussion of the proliferation of the Bible in print book culture, see Beal, *Rise and Fall*, 120–43.

3. *Das Newe Testament Deutzsch* (Wittenberg: Melchior Lotter for Christian Döring and Lucas Cranach, 1522). Courtesy of Special Collections at Emory University's Pitts Theological Library.

4. "Preface to the Revelation of John," in *Luther's Works 35: Word and Sacrament I*, ed. and trans. E. Theodore Bachmann (Philadelphia: Fortress Press, 1960), 398–99.

5. For an excellent overview of Lucas Cranach the Elder's life and work, esp. with Luther, see Stephan Füssel, "Cranach, Lucas the Elder," in *The Oxford Encyclopedia of the Bible and the Arts*, ed. Timothy Beal (New York: Oxford University Press, 2015), 1:246–51; and esp. Stephan Füssel, *The Bible in Pictures: Illustrations from the Workshop of Lucas Cranach (1534)—A Cultural Historical Introduction* (Cologne: Taschen, 2009). For a most thorough and insightful introduction to print Bible illustration more generally as it relates to Cranach and Luther's Bible, see David M. Gunn, "Bible Illustration," in Beal, *Bible and the Arts*, 2.1–22. My work here is especially indebted to Füssel and Gunn.

6. The two most notable printed German Bibles with illustrations before Luther's were those of Heinrich Quentell in Cologne (1478–79) and Anton Koberger in Nuremberg (1483), on which, see Gunn, "Illustration," 1–3.

7. Erwin Panofsky, *The Life and Art of Albrecht Dürer* (Princeton, NJ: Princeton University Press, 1955), 56; and the discussion in David H. Price, *Albrecht Dürer's Renaissance: Humanism, Reformation, and the Art of Faith* (Ann Arbor: University of Michigan Press, 2003), 62–64. See also "Dürer, Albrecht," in Beal, *Bible and the Arts*, 2:28 and 30–31. The text of Revelation in Dürer's work appeared in both the Latin Vulgate (*Apocalypsis cum figuris*) and German (*Die heimlich offenbarung*) in 1498.

8. Cranach does not include illustrations related to two of Dürer's: (1) the martyrdom of John and (7) the adoration of the Lamb. Those illustrations by Cranach that do not match any of Dürer's are: (4) the fifth seal, in which martyrs are raised from the dead and given white robes (Revelation 6:9–11; Dürer's fifth illustration includes the fifth and sixth seals together, and Cranach's next [sixth] illustration, depicting the sixth seal, is closer to that one); (8) the crowned locusts with scorpion's tails (Revelation 9:1–12); (11) the two witnesses being confronted by the beast (Revelation 11:3–7); (14) the Lamb on Mount Zion while an angel proclaims the Gospel (Revelation 14:1–8); (15) the winepress and reaping of divine wrath (Revelation 14:9–20); (16) the bowls of plagues (Revelation 16); (18) the fall of Babylon and mourning of kings and merchants (Revelation 18); (19) the defeat of the dragon and his armies; and (21) the new heaven, new earth, and new Jerusalem (Revelation 21).

9. Price, *Albrecht Dürer's Renaissance*, 30.

10. Füssel, "Cranach," 249.

11. Beal, *Rise and Fall*, 130.

12. On the publishing history of the September Testament, see Mark U. Edwards Jr., *Printing, Propaganda, and Martin Luther* (Philadelphia: Fortress Press, 1994), esp. 123–30; and Gunn, "Illustration," 6–8.

13. Gunn, "Illustration," 7.

14. I noted the concentration of wear and finger staining in Revelation in the 1522 edition of the September Testament as well as Luther's *Das Newe Testament*, bound together with *Die Propheten alle Deutsch* and *Apocrypha* (Leipzig: Nicolaus Wolrab, 1541) and a colorized edition of Luther's *Biblia* (Nuremberg: Johann vom Berg and Ulrich Newber, 1550), all courtesy of Special Collections at Emory University's Pitts Theological Library.

15. *Biblia: beider Allt unnd Newen Testamenten*, trans. J. Johan Dietenberger (Mainz: Peter Jordan, 1534). The twenty-one woodcuts for Revelation by Hans Sebald Beham and Anton Woensam are closer to Cranach than to Dürer (e.g., the first image of the "one like the son of man" has John prostrate on the ground rather than kneeling, and the various other elements are nearly identical to Cranach's). They also include those illustrations done by Cranach without precedent in Dürer (e.g., the locusts from the bottomless pit). Courtesy of Special Collections at Emory University's Pitts Theological Library.

CHAPTER 7. NEW WORLD OF GODS AND
MONSTERS: OTHERING OTHER RELIGIONS

1. Gordon W. Prange, *Hitler's Words: Two Decades of NS, 1923–1943* (Washington, DC: American Council on Public Affairs, 1944), 89; cited in David Sikkink and Mark Regnerus, "For God and Fatherland:

Protestant Symbolic Worlds and the Rise of German National Socialism," in *Disruptive Religion: The Force of Faith in Social-Movement Activism*, ed. Christian Smith (New York: Routledge, 1996), 159. See also Elaine Pagels, *Revelations: Visions, Prophecy, and Politics in the Book of Revelation* (New York: Viking, 2012), 38; citing Richard Steigmann-Gall, *The Holy Reich: Nazi Conceptions of Christianity, 1919–1945* (Cambridge: Cambridge University Press, 2003).

2. As Judith Kovacs and Christopher Rowland, *Revelation*, Blackwell Bible Commentaries (Oxford: Blackwell, 2004), 187, aptly put it with regard to the proliferation of the whore of Babylon, "the general connection is clearer than the detailed interpretation."

3. See chapter 5, note 13. David L. Barr, "Women in Myth and History: Deconstructing John's Characterizations," in *A Feminist Companion to the Apocalypse of John*, ed. Amy-Jill Levine with Maria Mayo Robbins (New York: T & T Clark, 2009), 55–68, argues that all the female figures in Revelation are "symbolic constructs" rooted in mythological figures. The whore of Babylon, he argues, is rooted in the ancient Near Eastern chaos mother god Tiamat, which suggests fascinating potential connections between her and the dragon (as well as Gaia, "Earth," who swallows the river pouring from the dragon's mouth in 12:16). For discussions of ancient Near Eastern chaos monsters, especially Babylonian and Canaanite ones, along with a fuller unpacking of the linguistic genealogies that connect them, the Hebrew biblical figures of Leviathan, Yamm, and *tannin* ("sea monster"), and John's

dragon, see Timothy Beal, *Religion and Its Monsters* (New York: Routledge, 2001), ch. 1, 2, and 6, which I summarize here.

4. Seamus Heaney, *Beowulf: A New Verse Translation*, bilingual ed. (New York: Farrar, Straus and Giroux, 2000), ll. 2326–27. For a fuller discussion of the biblical dimensions of the monsters in Beowulf, see Timothy Beal, "Beowulf," in *The Oxford Encyclopedia of the Bible and the Arts*, ed. Timothy Beal (New York: Oxford University Press, 2015), 1:89–93.

5. On these and other early monstrocizings in European art, see esp. Partha Mitter, *Much Maligned Monsters: A History of European Reactions to Indian Art* (Chicago: University of Chicago Press, 1977 and 1992), esp. 1–28, upon which I am drawing extensively. See also my discussion in *Religion and Its Monsters*, 103–22.

6. Mitter, *Much Maligned Monsters*, 12.

7. *The Itinerary of Lodovico de Varthema of Bologna from 1502–1508*, trans. John Winter Jones, ed. N. M. Penzer (London: Argonaut Press, 1928), 55–56. Varthema's *Itinerario* was first published in 1510 in Italian, and then translated into Latin in 1511. Jones's translation, quoted here, is from the original Italian. Richard Eden's 1577 English translation, *The Navigation and Voyages of Lewis Wetomannus*, was based on the Latin.

8. Mitter, *Much Maligned Monsters*, 17–18.

9. For an attempt at reconstructing what Indian figures may have been in this chapel, see esp. Jennifer Spinks, "The Southern Indian 'Devil in Calicut' in Early Modern Northern Europe: Images, Texts and Objects in Motion," *Journal of Early Modern History* 18 (2014): 15–48.

10. Jörg Breu, "Idol von Calicut," woodcut, in Ludovico de Varthema, *Die Ritterlich und lobwürdig Reisz* (Strassburg, 1516), http://www.musethno.uzh.ch /static/html/de/ausstellungen/2005/Blick_nach _Indien/Pressebilder/pressebilder.html. On Breu's religious and political history, Pia F. Cuneo, *Art and Politics in Early Modern Germany: Jörg Breu the Elder and the Fashioning of Political Identity ca. 1475–1536* (Leiden: Brill, 1998), 15–81.

11. *The Voyage of John Huyghen van Linschoten to the East Indies: From the Old English Translation of 1598*, trans. Arthur Coke Burnell (London: Hakluyt Society, 1885), 1:296–97. Burnell indicates that the Dutch text describes the teeth hanging over the chin rather than down to the knees.

12. European representations of human sacrifice and of Indian gods devouring people may also allude to another biblical figure of religious otherness: Molech, a god identified with human sacrifice in several passages of the Hebrew Bible. Molech is a rival to the biblical God that is mentioned primarily in the context of prohibitions against child sacrifice (2 Kings 23:10; Leviticus 18:21 and 20:2-5; 1 Kings 11:7, Jeremiah 32:35; Acts 7:43). See the discussion in George C. Heider, *The Cult of Molech: A Reassessment* (Sheffield: Sheffield Academic Press, 1985); and John Day, *Molech: A God of Human Sacrifice in the Old Testament* (Cambridge: Cambridge University Press, 1990).

13. Homi K. Bhabha, *The Location of Culture* (London and New York: Routledge, 1994), 70–71. Stephen D. Moore's essay, "Mimicry and Monstrosity," in *Untold*

Tales from the Book of Revelation: Sex and Gender,
Empire and Ecology (Atlanta: Society of Biblical
Literature, 2014), 13–38, in conversation with
Bhabha's critical categories of colonial ambivalence,
hybridity, and mimicry, identifies a similar dynamic
within the text of Revelation itself with regard to the
Roman empire: in its envisioned supersession of that
empire by a heavenly one, to what extent is it ultimately reinscribing rather than resisting that imperial
ideology?

14. Lucy Evangeline Guinness, *Across India at the Dawn of
the 20th Century* (Religious Tract Society, 1898), 199.

15. Guinness's proclamation that "thy shame is public" is
also reminiscent of the violent shaming of Babylon,
personified as a woman, in Revelation 18 (see also
Ezekiel 16 and Jeremiah 13).

16. In the United States, the most significant increases in
immigration from Asia have come since the Immigration and Nationality Act of 1965, which repealed
the earlier quota system that had linked immigration
numbers to ethnic populations already established in
the United States. On the rise of the Christian right
since around that same time, see esp. Steven P. Miller,
The Age of Evangelicalism (New York: Oxford University Press, 2014).

17. Pat Robertson, *Answers to 200 of Life's Most Probing
Questions* (Nashville, TN: Thomas Nelson, 1984), 142.
See also Ken Philpott, *A Manual of Demonology and
the Occult* (Grand Rapids, MI: Zondervan, 1976), 137,
138, and 163.

18. E.g., Pat Robertson, *The New World Order* (Dallas:
Word Publishing, 1991).

19. Janet I. Tu, "Yoga 'Demonic'? Critics Call Ministers' Warning a Stretch," *The Seattle Times*, October 11, 2010, http://www.seattletimes.com/seattle-news/yoga-demonic-critics-call-ministers-warning-a-stretch.

20. Beth Eckert, video testimonial on http://theotherside ofdarkness.com; Czarina Ong, "Witch-Turned-Christian Says There Is a Connection Between Yoga and Satan," *Christianity Today*, December 18, 2016, http://www.christiantoday.com/article/witch.turned .christian.says.there.is.a.connection.between.yoga.and .satan/103088.htm. See also the article on Virginia lieutenant gubernatorial candidate and pastor E. W. Jackson by Garance Franke-Ruta, "GOP Candidate: Yoga Opens You to Satanic Possession," *The Atlantic Monthly*, June 5, 2013, https://www.theatlantic.com /politics/archive/2013/06/gop-candidate-yoga-opens -you-to-satanic-possession/276570/.

21. Alison Lesley, "Catholic Priest Links Yoga and Satan During Satanism Sermon," *World Religion News*, March 6, 2015, http://www.worldreligionnews.com /issues/catholic-priest-links-yoga-satan-satanism -sermon.

22. Augustine, *The City of God*, trans. Marcus Dods, in *Nicene and Post-Nicene Fathers of the Christian Church*, ed. Philip Schaff (Edinburgh: T & T Clark), 2:20.7; 2:18.31.

23. An early example of this prevalent Christian idea of the "kingdom of darkness" as a diabolically seductive place to which one may lose one's salvation is the fourth and final part of Thomas Hobbes's *Leviathan or The Matter, Forme and Power of a Common Wealth Ecclesiasticall and Civil* (London, 1651) entitled "Of

the Kingdom of Darkness." Here he speaks not only of spiritual darkness from ignorance but also of "a Confederacy of Deceivers" which go under the various names of Satan, demons, phantasms, and spirits of illusion (333). See also the illustrated catalogue of demons and monsters written by Nathaniel Crouch under the pseudonym Robert Burton, *The Kingdom of Darkness* (London: A. Bettesworth and J. Batley, 1728).

24. Corinna Craft, "Testimony of Deliverance from a Demon of Yoga," *Deep Healing International*, http://www.deephealing.eu/index.php/do-more/articles/13 -testimony-of-deliverance-from-a-demon-of-yoga.

CHAPTER 8. HEAVEN IN A GARAGE: JAMES HAMPTON'S THRONE ROOM

1. Biographical information about Hampton is drawn from "James Hampton," Smithsonian American Art Museum, available at http://americanart.si.edu; Lynda Roscoe Hartigan, "Going Urban: American Folk Art and the Great Migration," *American Art* 14.2 (2000), 26–51; Hartigan, "The Throne of the Third Heaven of the Nation's Millennium General Assembly," originally published by the Museum of Fine Arts, Boston, for a 1976 exhibition of James Hampton's work, and now available at http://www.fredweaver .com/throne/throneessay.html. Quotations and details of the discovery of Hampton's throne room are from To Thompson, "The Throne of the Third Heaven of the Nations Millenium [*sic*] General Assembly," *The Washington Post*, August 9, 1981; and Paul Richard, "A Throne of Faith: Visionary Folk Art," *The Washington Post*, December 6, 1977.

2. Hartigan, "The Throne Room."

3. Stephen Jay Gould, "James Hampton's Throne and the Dual Nature of Time," *Smithsonian Studies in American Art* 1.1 (1987): 46–57.

CHAPTER 9. LEFT BEHIND AGAIN

1. Larry Norman's song, "I Wish We'd All Been Ready," first appeared on his album, *Upon the Rock* (Capitol, 1969).

2. *A Thief in the Night*, directed by Donald W. Thompson; written by Donald W. Thompson and Russell S. Doughten Jr. (16 mm film; Des Moines, IA: Mark IV Productions, 1972). Although the catalogued date of release is 1972, the date given in the opening titles is 1973.

3. This historical overview is based primarily on Joel A. Carpenter, *Revive Us Again: The Reawakening of American Fundamentalism* (New York: Oxford University Press, 1997). For a fuller discussion of the evangelical dilemma of popularization and preservation as it relates to the rise of Christian pop culture in the 1960s and 1970s, see Timothy Beal, *The Rise and Fall of the Bible: The Unexpected History of an Accidental Book* (New York: Houghton Mifflin Harcourt, 2011), 70–78; also 10–18.

4. See also Hal Lindsey, *Satan Is Alive and Well on Planet Earth*, with Carole C. Carlson (Grand Rapids, MI: Zondervan, 1972); Lindsey, *There's a New World Coming: An In-Depth Analysis of the Book of Revelation* (Eugene, OR: Harvest House, 1973).

5. As Brian Blount makes clear, John in Revelation by no means imagines believers being "spirited off to a safe

heavenly realm while conflict on a cosmic scale erupts on earth" (*Revelation*, 349). On the contrary, he fully expects them to undergo all of the ordeals that everyone else undergoes. This view is also clearly expressed and unpacked in great detail, as we saw, in Augustine's *City of God*.

6. The history of independent Christian filmmaking is well documented in Terry Lindvall, *Sanctuary Cinema: Origins of the Christian Film Industry* (New York: New York University Press, 2007), and Terry Lindvall and Andrew Quicke, *Celluloid Sermons: The Emergence of the Christian Film Industry, 1930–1986* (New York: New York University Press, 2011). My focus here is part of Lindvall and Quicke's second era in Christian independent filmmaking, the "16mm sound era" (40–46).

7. Baptista Film Mission–Collection 225 in the Billy Graham Center Archives of Wheaton College, http://www2.wheaton.edu/bgc/archives/GUIDES /225.htm.

8. Doughten's estimate in his commentary on the DVD of *A Thief in the Night* was 100 million, but by the time of his death he was estimating 300 million. This higher number has been picked up in most articles and popular news media since.

9. Heather Hendershot, *Shaking the World for Jesus: Media and Conservative Evangelical Culture* (Chicago: University of Chicago Press, 2004), 188.

10. Likewise the film's narrative framing strategy, which begins and ends with the exact same footage depicting our main character, Patty, waking up to being left behind by her recently converted husband while the radio explains what has happened. This is reminiscent

of the equally slow-moving and creepy *Carnival of Souls* (1962), a low-budget horror movie produced, cowritten, and directed by Herk Harvey, who was known for industrial films and commercials that have a similarly surprising ending that loops back to the beginning.

11. E.g., Lindsey, *There's a New World Coming*, 8.

12. The phrase also occurs in Matthew 24:36–44. Cf. Luke 12:39; 1 Thessalonians 5:2, 4; 2 Peter 3:10.

13. Lindvall and Quicke, *Celluloid Sermons*; Hendershot, *Shaking the World for Jesus*.

14. Thus these films adapt wholeheartedly to the familiar Hollywood mythos of the individual (almost always male) protagonist who must survive and overcome seemingly insurmountable obstacles, triumphing over evil not only by faith but also by courage and skill. On this Hollywood myth and the Christian film industry's conflicted relationship to it, see Lindvall, *Sanctuary Cinema*, 24.

15. "A71 Takes Soska Sisters' Remake of David Cronenberg's 'Rabid' for Canada," *The Hollywood Reporter*, November 5, 2017, https://www.hollywoodreporter .com/news/a71-takes-soska-sisters-remake-david -cronenbergs-rabid-canada-afm-2017-1055013.

16. As Kim Paffenroth points out in *The Gospel of the Living Dead: George Romero's Vision of Hell on Earth* (Waco, TX: Baylor University Press, 2006), zombies appear to be modeled on the image of the damned in Dante's *Inferno*, where he describes them as "the suffering race of souls who lost the good of intellect" (quoted on 22) and thus are, as Paffenroth puts it, "reduced just to appetite" (23).

17. *The Walking Dead*, "Beside the Dying Fire," season 2, episode 13, directed by Ernest Dickerson, written by Robert Kirkman and Glen Mazzara, *American Movie Channel*, March 18, 2012. For fuller studies of zombie culture vis-à-vis apocalypticism, Revelation, and other biblical texts, see especially Kelly J. Murphy, "The End Is (Still) All Around: The Zombie and Contemporary Apocalyptic Thought," in *Apocalypses in Context: Apocalyptic Currents through History*, ed. Murphy and Justin Jeffcoat Schedtler (Minneapolis, MN: Fortress Press, 2016); and David Pagano, "The Space of Apocalypse in Zombie Cinema," in *Zombie Culture: Autopsies of the Living Dead*, ed. Shawn McIntosh and Marc Leverette (Lanham, MD: Scarecrow Press, 2008).

CHAPTER 10. POST SCRIPT

1. Stephen D. Moore, *Untold Tales from the Book of Revelation: Sex and Gender, Empire and Ecology* (Atlanta: Society of Biblical Literature, 2014), 1.

2. Catherine Keller, *Apocalypse Now and Then: A Feminist Guide to the End of the World* (Boston: Beacon, 1996).

3. Ibid., 12–13.

4. Ibid., 11.

5. Matthew Gabriele, "Trump's Recognition of Jerusalem Excites Apocalyptic Fervor," *Religion News Service*, December 11, 2017, http://religionnews.com/2017/12/11/trumps-recognition-of-jerusalem-excites-apocalyptic-fervor/.

6. A simple Internet search for either name along with "666" or "Antichrist" is ample evidence. See, e.g.,

"One in Four Americans Think Obama May Be the Antichrist," *The Guardian*, April 2, 2013, https://www .theguardian.com/world/2013/apr/02/americans -obama-anti-christ-conspiracy-theories; and Tom Evans, "Is Trump REALLY the Antichrist? The Donald's Terrifying 666 Pattern REVEALED," *The Daily Star*, January 19, 2017, http://www.dailystar.co.uk/news/latest -news/563055/Donald-Trump-antichrist-satan-666 -pattern-president-elect-Hillary-Clinton-occult-devil.

7. https://www.facebook.com/groups /120615859280850I. On this and other similar groups, see Leanna Garfield, "Trump Has Caused a Growing Number of Liberals to Start Preparing for an Apocalypse," *Business Insider*, March 4, 2017, http:// www.businessinsider.com/liberal-doomsday-preppers -trump-2017-3.

8. The Guess Who, "American Woman," 7-inch single, written by Burton Cummings, Garry Peterson, Jim Kale, and Randy Bachman (RCA Victor, 1970).

9. Black Sabbath, "War Pigs," *Paranoid*, LP album, written by Tony Iommi, Ozzy Osbourne, Geezer Butler, and Bill Ward (Vertigo, 1970).

10. "War capitalism" is the apt renaming of "mercantile capitalism" in Sven Beckert, *Empire of Cotton: A Global History* (New York: Alfred A. Knopf, 2014).

11. Timothy Beal, *The Rise and Fall of the Bible: The Unexpected History of an Accidental Book* (New York: Houghton Mifflin Harcourt, 2011), 29–36.

12. Mary Shelley, *Frankenstein*, ed. J. Paul Hunter, Norton Critical Edition (New York: W. W. Norton, 2012), xii.

Dante, 96

Darby, John Nelson, 170, 177

Dawkins, Richard. *See* meme

December Testament, 135; *see also* September Testament *and* Luther's Bible

Denney, Alice, 156

Devil. *See* Satan

Dietenberger's German Bible, 136–37, 245n15

Diocletian, Emperor, 49–50

Dionysius of Alexandria, 2, 41–42, 52,

dispensationalism, 82, 114–16, 169–71, 177, 191–92

dominion script, 204–7; *see also* apocalypse script

Domitian, Emperor, 37–40, 229n9, 229n10, 229n11, 230n11; temple of, 39–40

Doughten, Russell S., 182, 183–84, 185–86, 188, 253n8

dragon, 140–41, 241n11; *see also* red dragon

Driscoll, Mark, 149

Dürer, Albrecht, 124–30, 244n7

early Jesus movement, diversity and conflict within, 43–45

early manuscripts of Revelation, 6–8

Eastwood, Clint, 32

Edict of Milan, 50

Eisenbaum, Pamela, 43, 230n17

Ephesus, 13, 39–40, 41

Erasmus, 7, 120

Esther, biblical book of, 99

Eusebius of Caesaria, 2–3, 38, 39, 40–42, 49–50, 52–53, 117, 229n10, 230n11,

evangelical pop culture, rise of, 175–77

evangelical rapture adventure, 191–93

evangelical rapture horror, 179–80, 191

Explo '72, 176–77

Ezekiel, biblical book of, 8, 45, 57, 72, 80–81, 97–99, 140, 240n7, 241n11, 249n15

Ezra, biblical book of, 99

Facebook, 202–3

feminist biblical criticism of Revelation, 3; Catherine Keller and, 200–201; by Tina Pippin and, 226n12; David Barr and, 246n3

Fiorenza, Elisabeth Schüssler, 3,

four horsemen, 4, 16

four living creatures, 14–16, 17, 23, 25, 31, 90, 92, 97–99, 161, 240n7,

Frankenstein, Mary Shelley's, 9–10, 48, 208

Frankfurter, David, 231n18

Frederick the Wise, 123

Fredriksen, Paula, 58

fundamentalism, Christian, xii, 58, 116, 170, 177–79, 252n3

Füssel, Stephan, 243n5

Gabrielle, Matthew, 201–2

Galatians, Paul's letter to, 44–45

Gebeno of Eberbach, 91, 94

generative incomprehensibility, 30–31, 88, 92, 138–39,

Genesis, biblical book of, 67, 68–69, 78, 84, 99, 169, 205, 206–7,

Geneva Bible, 7, 134, 139

George the Bearded, 134

German Bibles published before Luther's, 124

Gessius Florus, 34–35

God of Calicut, 143–45

Gospel of John, 40, 41–42, 116

Gospels, New Testament, 99

Gould, Stephen Jay, 168–69

grapes of wrath, 4, 23

Grendel, 141

Guinness, Lucy Evangeline, 147–48, 249n15

Gunn, David M., 243n5, 243n6

Hampton, James, 155–73

Hartigan, Lynda Roscoe, 251n1

Hebrew, biblical book of, 121

Hemenway, Michael, 8, 240n10

Herod Agrippa II, 34–35

hexakosioihexekontahexaphobia. *See* 666

Hildegard of Bingen, 73–93, 94, 95, 96, 114, 235n6, 236n12, 236n14, 237n15, 237n16, 237n19

Hirsch-Reich, Beatrice, 107, 238n2

Hitler, Adolf, 139

Hobbes, Thomas, 250n23

Huber, Lynn R., 225n8

Hydra, 140

hymns, Christian, xv

Instagram, 8

intertextuality, 47

Iraq, x

Irenaeus, 38–39, 40, 52, 226n11, 229n10, 230n11

Isaiah, biblical book of, 8, 45, 140, 233n12, 241n11

James, biblical letter of, 121

Jehovah's Witness, xv, 138

Jenkins, Jerry B., 191, 194

Jeremiah, biblical book of, 91

Jerome, 118

Jerusalem temple, second 1, 33, 35–37, 99, 229n11; first, 37, 229n8, 229n11; Ezekiel's vision of, 80; apocalyptic restoration of, 202

Jerusalem, 1, 19, 33–37, 43, 72, 99, 105, 201, 226n11, 226n12, 227n1, 229n11, ; *see also* new Jerusalem

Jewish Scriptures, 8, 45, 48, 140, 208; *see also* Old Testament

Jewish war against Rome (66–70 CE), 33–37

Jezebel, 14, 226n11

Joachim of Fiore, 73, 82, 93–116, 166, 169–70, 172, 235n6, 238n1, 238n2, 239n6, 241n13, 242n17, 242n20

Job, biblical book of, 99, 103, 208, 242n11

John of Patmos, writer of Revelation, 9, 32–33, 37–39, 42–48, 49, 79, 144, 208, ; as distinct from John, disciple of Jesus, 40–42

Paul, in contrast to John of Patmos, 43–45
Pentecostalism, xv
Pergamum, 13, 40
persecution, religious, 31, 37, 38–39, 49–50, 58, 64–65, 71, 86–88, 103–5, 134, 178, 227n3, 230n11, 233n10
Philo of Alexandria, 33–34, 227n2
Pippin, 3, 226n12
Pliny the Younger, 37, 229n9
Pope Eugenius III, 91
Pope Gregory VII, 134
Price, David, 133, 244n7
print book culture, media revolution of, 117–19; twilight of, 198
prophecy, Hebrew biblical, influence of, 8, 25, 45–47, 71, 73, 78, 79, 90, 140, 167, 201, 226, 234n1; *see also* Ezekiel, Isaiah, *and* Daniel
Psalms, 78, 103, 106, 140, 233n12,
Python, 140

Queen Mary, 134
queer studies and Revelation, 221n2
Quicke, Andrew, 253n6

rapture, the, x–xi, 10, 175–77, 199, 201, 206, ; and Bible, 177–79; and early Christian film, 179–80; and *A Thief in the Night*, 180–88; and *Left Behind*, 191–93; and zombie

apocalypses, 193–97; and theological horror, 197
Reagan, Ronald and Nancy, xii–xiii, 139
reception history, 221n3
red dragon, 2, 4, 11, 20–21, 100, 101–7, 108, 110, 140, 141, 241n11,
Reeves, Marjorie, 107, 238n2
Reformation, Protestant, 3, 78, 119, 120, 121, 134–35
Relfe, Mary Stewart, viii–ix, 219n2
resurrection of the dead, xv, 4, 26–27, 59–60, 61–63, 65–68, 69, 88, 91, 150, 163, 165, 172, 196, 197, 233n11,
revelationem / revelare, Latin meaning of, 113, 220n1, 242n19
Rilke, Rainer Maria, 133
Robertson, Pat, 149
Roman Catholic Church, the, xv, 51, 84–88, 118, 120, 121, 136–37, 150, d ; anti-Catholicism and, xv, 133–36, 138
Roman Empire, 1, 33–40, 43, 46, 49–52, 53, 58, 228n3, 229n11
Rowland, Christopher, 220n8, 246n2

Sacks, Oliver, 76
Saint George, 140
Saladin (Salah ad-Din Yusuf ibn Ayyub), 104–5
Satan, xii, xiii, xiv, 11, 14, 20–21, 26, 27, 40, 44, 50, 59–60, 63, 64–65, 71, 80, 103, 140, 143–47,